D0046007

The Cobra in the Barn

The Cobra in the Barn

Great Stories of
Automotive Archaeology

TOM COTTER

FOREWORD BY **PETER EGAN**

MOTORBOOKS

First published in 2005 by Motorbooks, an imprint of MBI Publishing Company, Galtier Plaza, Suite 200, 380 Jackson Street, St. Paul, MN 55101-3885 USA

© Tom Cotter, 2005

All rights reserved. With the exception of quoting brief passages for the purposes of review, no part of this publication may be reproduced without prior written permission from the Publisher.

The information in this book is true and complete to the best of our knowledge. All recommendations are made without any guarantee on the part of the author or Publisher, who also disclaim any liability incurred in connection with the use of this data or specific details. We recognize that some words, model names, and designations mentioned herein are the property of the trademark holder. We use them for identification purposes only.

Motorbooks titles are also available at discounts in bulk quantity for industrial or sales-promotional use. For details write to Special Sales Manager at MBI Publishing Company, Galtier Plaza, Suite 200, 380 Jackson Street, St. Paul, MN 55101-3885 USA.

ISBN-13: 978-0-7603-1992-5
ISBN-10: 0-7603-1992-8

Editors: Lee Klancher and Leah Noel
Layout Design: LeAnn Kuhlmann

Printed in China

On the front cover:
Top: A lifelong love of Lincolns led John Walcek to buy this 1941 Lincoln Continental Cabriolet out of a garage in northern California. *John Walcek*

Bottom: Cobra CSX2149 peaks out of a barn near Indianapolis, Indiana. It was first "discovered" (after being stored there for 30 years) when a propane gas delivery man spotted it. *Jim Maxwell*

On the back cover:
Walcek raises his hands in triumph—he has completed his quest of buying a great 1940s-era Lincoln. *John Walcek*

On the back cover flap:
Top: Author Tom Cotter at eighteen months old in his first car, a Champion pedal car that he called a T-Bird. *Johanna Skiebe Cotter McCloskey*

Bottom: Six hours into the disassembly of Cobra CSX2149.

Dedication

To the Skiebe sisters—Mom and Aunt Kiki—from whom
I inherited my "car genes," and of course my friend X,
with whom I first went searching for old cars. R.I.P.

Contents

CONTENTS

Acknowledgments

The author wishes to thank the following individuals for their assistance, patience, kindness, and support with this book: Kris Palmer, Lee Klancher, Peter Egan, Ken Gross, April Marie Drum, Pat Cotter, Brian Cotter, Leigh Dorrington, and everyone who submitted a barn-find story, whether it was used or not.

If you helped in some way and I have omitted your name, please know that I am grateful.

Foreword

BY PETER EGAN

F inding a desirable, old, abandoned car in a half-forgotten barn—it's one of the most potent dreams in the automotive world. Notice here that I used the word *desirable*.

Unfortunately, used car lots, farm fields, and barns are filled with cars that no one cared about very much when they were new, and time hasn't added a gilt of value and glamour to their ordinariness. As my old friend Allan Girdler once said, "An old six-cylinder Cranbrook doesn't get better looking, faster, or more valuable, just because it's worn out and parked in the weeds."

Or maybe it does. If you passed your driver's test in that Cranbrook, or drove it to the prom with your high school sweetheart, it might possess a peculiar value and magical quality elusive to others. With most old cars, beauty is in the eye of the once-teenage beholder who is now grown up and has money to spend.

But when most people dream about barn cars, they usually see visions of MGTCs, Bugatti Type 35Bs, finned Caddys, Jag XK120s, Packard Twin Sixes, Cobras, and so on—cars loved and admired when they were new, and still sought after today. Real classics, covered with pigeon droppings and straw, slumbering behind the Ford 8N tractor in that far corner of the barn where only a few stray beams of light fall on the dusty curve of the rear fender.

A romantic vision, to be sure.

But what, exactly, is so great about finding those legendary old cars in barns, rather than buying one that's polished, tuned, and ready to go at the classic car auction, or in the hands of an appreciative owner?

Part of it, I think, is the allure of the bargain. We hope (somewhat amorally) that the car's very neglect is a sign of addle-brained detachment on the part of the owner, reflecting a provincial, behind-the-times unawareness of the car's current market value.

"My husband left this little blue French car in the horse barn just before he ran off with that fan-dancer from Omaha. I just want it out of here." That sort of thing.

Unfortunately, my own experience has been that people who know absolutely nothing about cars tend to *overvalue* the tired old iron sitting in their barns and garages. ("Fifty dollars! Are you kidding? These rusty old Fiats are getting rare!") In most cases, you're much more likely to get a fair and realistic price from someone who knows exactly what the car is worth.

The real bargain factor, of course, lies in the car's neglect. Can't afford a freshly restored Series 1 E-Type roadster? Maybe you can find one in a barn somewhere that needs work. The low purchase price is merely the foot in the door that allows you—after years of knuckle-busting restoration work—to own a classic you couldn't afford to buy outright. I've used this "logic" in buying at least a dozen cars—never mind that they all ended up costing me a lot more than the nicest example on Earth, had I simply paid the going rate.

But to look too closely at all these economic factors is to miss the whole point of finding a car in a barn and dragging it home. The idea is not so much to score a bargain, but to find a favorite old car and bring it back to life. To free up the brakes, make the wheels turn, crank the engine, and hear combustion; to let the car roll out into the sunlight again and do what it was supposed to do, which is carry happy, mechanically mesmerized people down a scenic country road.

Finding that car in a barn and making it run again are as close as most car buffs will ever get to God, as depicted on the ceiling of the Sistine Chapel passing the spark of life to Adam. Or maybe a more appropriate and less grandiose image comes from stories by the Brothers Grimm, in which the earnest suitor passes many difficult tests and eventually kisses the sleeping princess, which brings her back to life.

Either way, it's hard to imagine a more romantic and compelling path to car ownership.

I would have to say that Tom Cotter, of all the people I've

worked and traveled with, is the most qualified to chronicle that romance and compulsion.

Tom lives, thinks, reads, and breathes old cars more deeply than anyone I know. He collects, searches, restores, judges at concours events, and goes far out of his way to help friends (such as yours truly) find the old cars they're looking for. He loves the hunt, and he's also a fast and dedicated racer of vintage sports cars.

A few years ago, I flew out to the San Francisco Bay area, met Tom at the airport, and helped him drive his newly purchased, very original red 1964 289 Cobra across the United States, all the way back to his home in North Carolina. The trip took us about a week, and we never even tried to put the top up. It was a good thing, too, because we later discovered the top had disintegrated in the trunk, from heat and old age.

I'm sorry to say this car didn't actually come out of a barn—it lived in the neat three-car garage of its knowledgeable and sympathetic owner—but it hadn't been driven much in recent years and it needed a little roadside wrenching to make the trip. Nothing disastrous, mind you, just the stuff of good adventure.

The trip was filled with great memories, but my favorite moment came when we were cruising through a small town on the plains of eastern Colorado.

As we drove through the center of this little burg, Tom's head swiveled slowly back and forth like a radar dish, sweeping over the houses, fences, backyards, and buildings. He suddenly turned to me, grinning, with a strange, maniacal gleam in his eye.

"Don't you wish," he said, "that you had X-ray vision so you could spot all the neat old cars that are probably hidden away in these small-town garages and old barns?"

Of course I did. I've had that very same thought a thousand times. We all have, even if we've never put it in words.

Well, Tom Cotter has finally put it in words—and pictures. And he's exactly the right guy for the job.

Peter Egan is a longtime automotive and motorcycle journalist. He has written his column, *Side Glances*, for *Road & Track* magazine since 1983. He is also an editor at large for *Cycle World* magazine.

Introduction

When Pat Huntley called to tell me her husband Stan had died, the news wasn't totally unexpected. He had been fighting colon cancer for a while and I knew he was nearing the end of his battle.

Yet one of Pat's words of comfort hit me hard. "Just know that Stan was so at peace with who the Sprite went to," she said.

I knew she was talking about me.

Just six months earlier, I had purchased Stan's beloved Austin-Healey Sprite Le Mans prototype coupe race car. Before that day, he had taken care of it for nearly thirty years in his Portland, Oregon, garage. So after he was diagnosed, I was lucky enough to be chosen as the famous race car's next "caretaker."

What later struck me the most about Pat's comment was that she had used the word peace—one not usually associated with finding and buying old cars, but one worth remembering. So many of the people I spoke to for this book told me that peace, or at least comfort, was often the only reason the longtime owner of a barn find would part with his cherished possession.

While the novice may think ownership is the best reward in barn finding, that's only partly true. The real joy lies in the search and discovery of these old cars. It is something that seems to reach back to our primal instincts. Who wouldn't want to find buried gold coins, left by Captain Cook, off some Caribbean Island? Or maybe untold riches left in a tomb by King Tut, or one of his cronies? But most car guys don't live on islands or in the desert, and they must deal with the "treasures" at hand.

For them, a potential jackpot lurks behind every barn door or fence.

One of the treasures I found was not too far from my home, in a lovely area of North Carolina called Davidson. For twenty years, I had driven by my next-door neighbor's farm, which had several barns that I fantasized were full of old cars. "But old cars are never next door," I kept telling myself. "That would be too easy."

Yet, remarkably, my neighbor Hugh did have a unique car in his barn—an A.C. Greyhound that rolled off the very same assembly line as my own A.C. Cobra! Imagine that, right next door!

Bill Warner, whose automotive exploits you'll read about in this book, shares a similar barn-find tale, one where he was also embarrassed to find a great car (a Lotus 11) just a stone's throw from his Jacksonville, Florida, home.

The best thing about this "automotive archaeology" is that it's fair game for everyone. There are no qualifications or price of entry. And there are still great cars to be found—"They're still out there!" my monthly Early Ford V-8 Club newsletter, *V-8 Times*, always proclaims.

"There are still some undiscovered Rolls-Royces, Bugattis, and Dueseys to be discovered," says Ritchie Cline, whose Imperial Palace Auto Collection in Las Vegas contains some of the world's great automotive treasures. "There are great cars sitting in little garages all over the world, still owned by guys who bought them thirty or forty years ago."

And these are closer than you'd think, it seems.

"Today, lots of cars are coming to our auctions that haven't been seen before," says Craig Jackson, promoter of the world's most successful automotive auction, says, "but the pre-war cars are running out. Yet like the Hemi Cuda convertible I found, there are still plenty of muscle cars to be found."

To find such a treasure, I recommend the following methods, all tested and proven effective:

1. Drive down dead-end streets. To most folks, a dead-end sign means having to make a three-point turn at the end of the road, which is a nuisance. But as Robert Frost said in his poem *The Road Less Traveled*, "because it was grassy and wanted wear," there are treasures waiting for you on those dead-end roads.

2. Go looking in winter. When leaves are off the trees, your vision through the "forest" of decaying garages and barns is better than ever. Suddenly, you might catch a peak of something hiding back behind all that junk.

3. Let everyone know you're a car nut. You'd be surprised how cars come out of the woodwork just by getting the word out.

After you hunt and find, then comes the hardest part of this dig—the purchase. It's like a dance, negotiating this precious jewel away from its longtime owner. Maybe you'll be really good at that part, like David Sydorick is. He's another car hunter profiled in this book and really knows how to give owners the peace of mind they want when selling their treasure away. In the end, you'll probably have to do what he does—prove to them the car is going to a good home. In the meantime, happy hunting.

—Tom Cotter
May 2005

CHAPTER ONE

Barn Finds

The Cobra in the Barn

In the United States, one car has appeared in almost every aspiring barn-finder's dreams: Shelby's legendary British-American hybrid. Mark Gardner, of San Clemente, California, saw this dream become reality when he heard about a rare car stowed in a large garage in Hawaii. It had sat untouched for three decades because its frustrated owner couldn't get the aluminum bodywork repaired correctly "on the Island." This was a lucky break for Gardner, for had the car been repaired, it probably would have been sold long before he found out about it.

According to the Shelby Registry, Cobra CSX2022 was the twenty-second Cobra manufactured, and it was invoiced to Shelby American in October 1962. It was delivered to Honolulu Ford in Hawaii and marked with a retail price of $5,346.65. It arrived in white paint with a red interior, an optional roll bar ($107), race tires, two seatbelts, and a cooling system rust inhibitor. Attorney Hyman

Greenstein purchased the car, campaigning it on sports car circuits with driver, Lloyd Sumaha. In October 1963, the car placed second in the production class in the Hawaiian Grand Prix.

Invoices from Shelby American show that the car was continually upgraded as new parts were developed. Greenstein added Goodyear Sports Car Special tires, a competition oil pan, an oil cooler kit, a racing windshield, a fiberglass hood scoop, four brake scoops, front and rear sway bars, replacement rear hubs, and a Harrison aluminum radiator.

At some point in its early life, the original 260-cubic-inch engine seized, and it was replaced with a HiPo 289. Shelby's Al Dowd sent a note to Greenstein explaining that the company had made a number of internal modifications to the 260, including reinforcing the oil pump tube. Greenstein's 260 lacked these improvements; with them, it may not have failed.

In 1967, Bob Brown, another Hawaiian resident, purchased the car from Greenstein. Brown loved Cobras, and he bought the car as his everyday driver, never knowing about its competition heritage. Only four months into Cobra ownership, while Brown was driving CSX2022 on the street, an oil line burst and the car erupted in

Unearthed after nearly four decades, CSX2022, the 22nd 289 Cobra built, is loaded onto a transporter in preparation for its cargo flight to San Diego. New bodywork, purchased from Shelby in the 1960s, went uninstalled when the owner could not find a welder capable of fitting the new panels properly. *Mark Gardner*

flames, damaging the front fenders, cowl, front seats, and dashboard. Disgusted, Brown parked the car in his garage with the intention of one day rebuilding it. He purchased two new front fenders and a cowl directly from Shelby, but when a local welder was unable to fit the pieces properly, Brown gave up. Time left the car all but forgotten in the back of his garage.

Then Gardner came along. Gardner had once lived in Hawaii (he now lives in California). While living there, he had mentioned to a mechanic friend that he really wanted to own a Cobra. The friend said he knew a gentleman who owned such a car and gave Gardner his phone number.

"Originally Bob Brown didn't want to talk to me," Gardner says. "But I'd call him every few months, just to say hello and remind him of my interest. Finally, one day in 2003 he called and said he could use the money, so he was ready to sell. I think what clinched it was my promise that once I had the car restored, he could come over and drive it up and down the Pacific Coast Highway to his heart's content."

Gardner wanted to fly to Hawaii to see the car in person, but he was discouraged by Brown, who said that his garage was a mess. So with complete trust, Gardner wired Brown an amount far below market value for a Cobra. Then he arranged to have an air freight company fly the car to California. In August 2003, Cobra CSX2022 left the garage where it had sat idle for more than thirty-five years.

Gardner purchased the car never knowing about its racing history. In fact, it wasn't until he had the Cobra at home that he purchased a copy of the Shelby Registry and learned of its early track career.

Goldmine!

"I called [Cobra collector and historian] Lynn Park, and we began to research the car. I brought the car to Steve Beckman of Costa Mesa," Gardner says. Beckman pulled off the aluminum body, set it aside, and Gardner went to work on refurbishing the chassis.

"The car has 18,000 miles, mostly race miles. Approximately 200 of those were put on by Brown," says Gardner. He also discovered that CSX2022 was raced with a variety of fuel systems, including a

Mark Gardner's Cobra is being restored in Steve Beckman's shop in Costa Mesa, California, after which it will be street driven and raced in vintage events. The promise of driving the completed car on the Pacific Coast Highway enticed the previous owner to sell. *Mark Gardner*

single four barrel, two four barrels, Webers, and Hilborn fuel injection. When he purchased the car, Gardner received all the intake systems except the fuel injection system.

CSX2022 also included the correct convertible top and side curtains. Since the car had been converted for racing, the top had never been used. A complete tool kit and jack came with the car as well. The car was equipped with Lucas headlights and Lucas driving lights.

The Cobra came from Shelby with wire wheels, but they had been converted to Halibrand kidney bean wheels early on in its racing life. At some point, those wheels were stolen, so it was on wire wheels when Gardner purchased it. Since then, with Park's help, Gardner has purchased a newly manufactured set of magnesium Halibrand-style wheels to install upon completion.

The car will be refinished in red with the original red interior. Even though it will be vintage raced, it will also be street legal.

And what was the price Gardner paid for one of the earliest independent competition Cobras in the world? $50,000. That should be encouraging to all treasure hunters out there.

Ferrari Dreams

Tom Farrell lives outside of Charlotte, North Carolina, in the land of NASCAR, muscle cars, and hot rods. All his friends drive Mustangs and Camaros, but he has always been more attracted to foreign cars and sports cars. "I always wanted to drive something a little bit different than all my friends drive," he says.

Farrell works as a model maker for Penske Racing South in Mooresville, North Carolina, in the wind tunnel and aerodynamics department. The team fields NASCAR Nextel Cup cars for drivers Rusty Wallace and Ryan Newman. As part of his job, Farrell can spend six to seven weeks crafting a forty-five-percent model to test in the wind tunnel. So obviously, he has the patience to restore an old car. He's also handy with a wrench, which he proved as part of

After two hours of moving household items from the top of the Ferrari, Tom Farrell was finally able to see the car he hoped to purchase. The 250 GTE had been parked in a Asheville, North Carolina, garage and had not moved for thirteen years. *Tom Farrell*

Penske South's winning *Junkyard Wars* team. With this combination of talents, all he needed to make his personal car dreams come true was a project he was interested in—and a lucky connection.

That connection came through Tom's friend Lance Hooper, a crew chief on a Craftsman Truck racing team, who was dating an Asheville woman, Lisa Jackson. Her father, Richard, was a one-time Winston Cup team owner who happened to have an old Ferrari—a fact that Hooper casually mentioned to Farrell one day, adding that the car "hasn't moved in thirteen years."

Farrell was all ears. "I'd always loved Ferraris, but never thought I'd be able to afford one," he says.

Eventually, he worked up the nerve to ask if he could look at the car. Lisa cleared it with her parents and Farrell grabbed his camera, jumped in his truck, and headed toward Asheville. "It took us two hours to uncover the car," he says. "It was a 1963 250 GTE, and had thirteen years of junk piled on it." He took a number of photos and said he'd be interested in buying if it was available.

After several months, he and Jackson had a phone conversation. Apparently Jackson had given the Ferrari to his wife after she had seen one like it. He had found the nice silver example at FAF Motors in Georgia and surprised her with the 6,700-mile cream puff. Eventually, the car was painted bright red, and his wife drove it with gusto. "I think Richard eventually took it away from his wife because she got too many speeding tickets in it," Farrell says. So it sat in the garage as years worth of household goods were piled on top of it.

If there was to be a sale, Jackson's wife would have to approve, and over the years, the couple had been approached by a number of Ferrari enthusiasts. Yet everyone who expressed interest in the car wanted to dismantle it and sell it for parts, which had a value greater than the car as a whole. Farrell convinced the Jackson family that his intentions were different: he had no desire to sell the car for parts. He had wanted a Ferrari for many years, and the purchase of this car would make his dream come true.

Farrell had a dialogue with the Jacksons over the next six months. During that time, he enlisted the expertise of the Ferrari Register's Len Miller. The register provides a listing of all Ferrari 250 models, ownership history, and other records. Miller told Farrell how much parts and service would cost, and together they came up with a range of value. Eventually, Jackson called Farrell and said he'd take $8,000 for the car. Farrell said he could only afford $7,000. Jackson accepted, and in less than three hours Farrell was sitting in Jackson's driveway with his trailer in tow.

"When I got the car home, I had to replace most of the upper engine gaskets because they all leaked so badly," Farrell says. "The good news was that the gas in the tank was still liquid—it hadn't turned to jelly—probably because Jackson had run racing fuel in the car, which doesn't go bad like pump gas."

After changing many engine gaskets and cleaning the fuel lines, Farrell, a Penske South scale-model builder, was able to put the Ferrari back on the road again. After winning a People's Choice Award at a Ferrari meet, he disassembled the car for restoration. *Tom Farrell*

Farrell did have to relocate some "residents" that had lived in the car during its lengthy storage life. "I found squirrel or rat nests in the glove compartment and under the hood insulation blanket," he says. "But overall, the car had a sound body." When he purchased the car, it had covered 25,000 miles.

It seems that the car was stored outside, probably at the race shop, for some time during those thirteen years. When it was trailered to Jackson's house, the brakes failed while it was being unloaded and the car rolled slowly into the edge of the garage. That explained the dented rear bumper.

Farrell drove the car for two years before disassembling it for restoration. On one last fling before taking it apart, he drove the car to a Ferrari Club of America show in North Carolina and won the People's Choice Award in 2004.

"When we started taking it apart, my six-year-old son Jared saw the old eight-track tape deck and asked what kind of video player it was," Farrell says, adding that his young son loves to work on the car.

The car is now disassembled, being returned to as-new condition. Even the red paint will give way to a fresh coat of the factory original silver. Not surprisingly, the restoration is taking much of Farrell's free time. "My wife hates the car," he says. "She says it's my girlfriend."

Lots of people in the Carolinas don't know what type of car his Ferrari is, so Farrell has some fun when he tells them it's a 1963 Ford Mustang, then shows them the prancing horse logo on the hood as "proof." He hopes to "fool" a few more people when the car is finally ready for summer cruising in 2005.

Fifty-Eight Cars for $1,500

It was a slow Friday afternoon when car collector Don Orosco began to talk about the car he wanted to track down. At three o'clock, he told his business partner that he would spend the rest of the day trying to find a car he had only recently heard about.

Of course, Orosco doesn't do anything in a small way; he has amassed a terrific collection of antique cars, sports cars, racing cars, and hot rods by applying the same tenacious principles to hunting down cars as he does in developing real estate.

He explains his start in automotive wheeling and dealing this way: "It was 1972, and I was working for Xerox, bored and barely making ends meet. But I was a car guy, and always wanted to make a living in the car business. So, after clearing it with my wife, I took an ad out in the *San Francisco Chronicle* for thirty-five dollars that read: 'Wanted–Model A Ford,' and gave my phone number. Then I went to my bank and asked them if I would be eligible for a credit line of $1,500. They said yes and, in fact, I could borrow up to $2,500, but I told them I only wanted $1,500. Well, guess how many cars I bought from that ad? Would you believe fifty-eight? I'd buy a Model A for $25, take off the parts I needed for my own, then sell it for $75. I was tripling my money. My wife thought I was a genius."

Three decades later, Orosco had gone from buying Model A Fords to accumulating some of the most prized collector cars in existence. The car he had heard about and decided to search for on that lazy Friday afternoon some years ago was a Porsche RS60/61 Spyder. The tip was as oblique as they come. The gentleman who had told him about the race car said that it was rumored to be in the upper Midwest, up near Nebraska, the Dakotas, Montana, Idaho, but beyond that, he couldn't give any more information.

Orosco dialed the Porsche Club representative for the state of Idaho, just to see if he had ever heard of the RS Porsche. "He told me that rumors of such a car had circulated among the club's members for years, but nobody had ever confirmed it. But he did tell me the car was thought to be in Idaho, and that the owner had a common last name, like Jones or Smith or Walters or Walker, and had a house in one of the bigger towns and another house down south in a rural part of the state. I said thanks and hung up."

In just four minutes, Orosco had gotten another confirmation on the rumored Porsche, confirmed Idaho as the state, and had a couple of leads on possible names and possible cities linked to the car. "My partner is looking at me on the phone, and he couldn't believe it," Orosco says.

Next, he called Idaho telephone information. "I asked the lady on the phone if she was having a good day, and she said yes, but it was Friday afternoon, and she was looking forward to the weekend," he says. "I asked her if she had the time to help me track down a person with a name like Smith or Jones or Walters or Walker, who had a house in one of the cities, and another to the south. She said that the task sounded interesting, and that she'd be glad to help. Within just a minute or two, she said that a man named Walker owned a home in Sun Valley, Idaho, and another near the state's southern border in Bliss. I said thank you very much, and hung up."

It was now 3:06 p.m., and Orosco picked up the phone to call a Mr. Archie Walker. "The phone rang once or twice, and a woman answered. I asked her if she was having a good day, and mentioned that I was looking for a certain person in Idaho, and that possibly she could help me. Then I asked her if she knew what a Porsche RS Spyder was. She said, 'Well, yes, I'm looking at one right now. It's my father's.'"

It was now 3:07, and in less than ten minutes, Orosco had tracked down a car that had eluded Porsche collectors for years. This was in the days before the Internet, so the discovery was made via telephone, a hunch, and some good luck.

Well, later that day, Orosco spoke with Mr. Walker personally. He asked if it would be okay if he came up to see the car. Mr. Walker said that would be fine, so flights were arranged. Interestingly, in another stroke of luck, one of the airlines had just begun nonstop service from San Francisco to Idaho that very week, so Orosco hopped on a jet, then rented a car, and began a sort of dream scavenger hunt. "My directions were to turn from the paved road onto a dirt road, take the third dirt road to the right, then turn left at the cactus, but eventually I found Mr. Walker's ranch," he says. "Mrs. Walker greeted me and led me to the barn at the rear of the house, where Mr. Walker was working on some old tractors. Seems he had been a Mercedes-Benz dealer in the Boise area, and bought the Porsche to run in club events on the weekends. Eventually he sold the dealership and moved his car out to his ranch, where it sat, covered with dust amid a bunch of huge John Deere tractors."

Mr. Walker was cordial to Orosco and let him inspect the car—which was a real, honest-to-God Porsche Spyder—but told him that unfortunately the Porsche was not for sale. Orosco left, somewhat disappointed, but pleased with his detective work. He did ask, though, that if Mr. Walker ever did decide to sell the Porsche, would he please call him first. Mr. Walker agreed.

A few months went by and Orosco forgot about the Porsche. Then Mr. Walker called him in his office. His wife wanted to buy a new Mercedes station wagon. (As a former dealer, Mr. Walker was still entitled to a discount.) He proposed a trade: If Orosco would provide enough funds for the new Mercedes station wagon, he could have the Porsche. "I think the Mercedes was about $28,000 to $30,000 at the time," Orosco says, "so I sent him a check, and the Porsche was mine."

As it turns out, Orosco's Porsche find had quite a checkered racing history. The car finished second in the 1960 twelve-hour endurance race at Sebring as a quasi-factory entry with drivers Bob Holbert, Roy Schecter, and Howard Fowler. It was fielded by Brumos Porsche of Jacksonville, Florida, and finished second to the official factory RS60 team C12 of Hans Hermann and Olivier Gendebien.

Over his lifetime as a car collector, Orosco has collected hundreds of barn-find stories, but his favorite, even after twenty years, is still his discovery of the elusive Porsche race car in an Idaho barn.

The Tomato Farm Jag

BY BILL SCHMIDT AND KRIS PALMER

People who own an exotic car often know where others like it may be found. They've met other owners when searching for their own car, or maybe through a local club. Drivers of exotic cars also hear from total strangers, who seek them out to tell them they know of another car "just like that one." That's the claim Bill Schmidt heard while driving his friend's Jaguar XK140.

His friend had brought the Jag to Bill's hometown of Sacramento because it had a tired engine, and he wanted to avoid the high repair prices in his own area—Orange County, California. Since Bill had always admired the car, and helped his friend save good money, Bill got a favor in return—being able to put some break-in miles on the Jaguar before it went back to Orange County.

Bill Schmidt loads his trailer with the 1951 XK120 Jaguar—finally out of the barn in Woodland, California. The previous owners, two brothers, painted the car, then abandoned their restoration effort beneath a tarp, letting it slowly rot from years of neglect and accumulated pigeon "loam." *Bill Schmidt*

When he was out in the car one day, a man called over to him at a stoplight. He said he had a friend with a car "just like that one" in a barn north of town. He thought the car's owner might be interested in selling it. Bill didn't know if the guy was right or wrong about the car, but he gave him his number just in case. The other driver said he'd pass it on next time he saw his friend with the barn.

A few days later, the driver called him with the phone number of the Jaguar XK's owner, who was teaching at a college in Washington state. Schmidt called the number and learned that the man did have an XK roadster, but wasn't interested in selling it right now. The car was older than Bill's friend's, and the owner still hoped to complete the restoration he felt the car (a 1951 XK120) deserved.

It wasn't an offer of sale, yet it wasn't a conclusive refusal either. Bill could sense the owner's willingness to part with the car—he just needed more time. He was nice guy, whom Schmidt didn't mind calling again. He did, every month or so, to bring up the subject of the stowed-away XK120. Finally the man suggested they get together when he came back to California at the end of the school year.

That August, the man called Bill and told him to meet him at the family tomato farm. It was a hot Sacramento day when Bill drove to the address the owner had specified. As Bill entered the property, he saw a mechanical picker lumbering between the rows of tomato vines while a crew rode along culling the fruit. The man's brother was on hand, too. He had taken over the farm.

The Jaguar was in a large barn nearby. It was sitting under some rotting tarps. Overhead, pigeons roosted in the rafters, doing what pigeons do. Their droppings had fallen on top of and around the car for the last seventeen years. It was hub-deep in loam.

The tarps provided only mediocre protection. Dust covered the car. It was so thick that Bill couldn't read the instrument faces. As they looked it over, the brothers told him that it had been their sister's car. She had raced it around the back farm roads for years until it needed work. Together with her brothers, they had taken the car apart, painted it, and then stuck it in the barn. Their plan

After the car was moved to a mechanic's shop in Sacramento, the cleanup process began. Mice nests were hidden throughout the car's interior, including under the dashboard and even in the exhaust pipe. *Bill Schmidt*

was to finish putting it back together as soon as time allowed. Seventeen years later, that moment had yet to arrive. In that time, the sister had moved away and other priorities kept her brothers from doing anything with the old Jaguar.

Beneath the tarps was a car partially dismantled, with parts tucked in and around it. The windshield was disassembled and resting in the trunk, along with the car's small bumpers. The grille was there, as were other bits removed when the car was painted with cream lacquer paint. Some nearby garbage bags held Pirelli tires and tubes, which the siblings planned to install as they finished the car. Only the hood appeared damaged. It had been dented when a storm blew the barn door into it. Fortunately, the brothers acquired a spare hood for the car, but like the tires, it had not been fitted.

Despite the dust and pigeon droppings, Schmidt liked what he saw. This was a sports icon and it seemed to be a complete car. He was ready to make an offer—but how much? It was the late 1980s and collector car values were on the rise. Bill was just finishing a Sunbeam Tiger restoration and his budget was lean for a car like this. He offered what he thought he could afford: $8,000. The brothers' reaction suggested they were hoping for more. Bill thanked them for their time and left the farm. He didn't expect to hear from the brothers again.

Late the following evening, a Sunday, the phone rang. It was the college professor. He said he'd accept the offer if Bill could sweeten it by $350. The friend who had told Bill about the car had fallen on hard times, and the Jaguar owner wanted to get him a little cash, for introducing them, to help him get by. Bill agreed and asked when he could pick it up. The owner said he wanted it gone the following day.

Schmidt made some quick phone calls and got a local Jaguar mechanic to accompany him the following day with a rented trailer. By the time they got there, the brothers had already filled the tires and pushed the car out into the sun. Bill and the mechanic got it

Schmidt and his mechanic squirted some oil in the cylinders, repaired some wiring, and hooked up a new battery. The $8,350 Jag then sputtered to life with a push of the starter button, launching the tailpipe's surprised rodent residents across the garage floor. *Bill Schmidt*

loaded, along with the spare hood and Pirellis, and took it to the mechanic's shop.

As they cleared dust and discovered parts, live mice darted from the nests they'd made in the car. When Bill grabbed a radiator hose, it crumbled. Apart from that, things looked pretty good. The mechanic said, "I think we can start it." He pulled the plugs, poured a bit of automatic transmission fluid into the cylinders, changed the oil, jury-rigged some wiring (the original harness was a mess), and hooked up a battery. He put some gas in the SU carburetors' bowls and hit the starter button. After about ten tries, the engine roared to life, spitting mice nests from the tailpipes across the garage. White smoke filled the bay. The engine ran until the gas in the bowls was gone.

Freed from its dusty abandonment, the XK120 was a runner again. Bill replaced the hoses, wiring, and brakes; fixed the radiator; and had the Pirelli tires mounted and balanced. Without its windshield fitted, the long, low car with its wheel spats looked more like a torpedo. The brakes pulled to the left sharply, but the gearbox was the best he'd felt in an early Jaguar. Though it could have used a valve job, the original engine ran fairly quiet and strong.

Bill took the Jaguar to a local car meet that summer, where it received more attention than well-restored cars. It was a great find, and a Jaguar enthusiast once chased him down and offered him $20,000 on the spot—more than twice what he'd spent on it. He refused that offer, but accepted a later one. Other priorities demanded Bill's time and resources, and he didn't feel he could give the car the restoration it deserved. With collector prices starting to fall in the early 1990s, he let it go to a Southern California collector for $17,000.

Bill retains pictures and fond memories of the car and wonders sometimes if it ever got the restoration he felt the car deserved. He has no regrets, however. In his view, the chase, and catch, is often more fun than actually owning the car.

A Propane Gas
Delivery Man's Discovery

Electric company meter-readers, landscapers, and other delivery-men possibly have the best opportunity to discover vehicles "just out of view" from car collectors. After all, they can venture onto properties, look behind bushes, and peer into barns. The story of Cobra CSX2149 begins this way, when a propane gas delivery driver looked into a customer's remote barn near Indianapolis, Indiana, in 1993.

What the deliveryman saw was a small sports car he believed was a Triumph or an MG. He mentioned the discovery to a friend, who mentioned it to a friend, who then told his young cousin. We'll call this cousin Johnny.

Well, being an enterprising youth, Johnny knocked on the owner's door and asked if he could please see the sports car. Opening the barn doors and climbing behind tractors, cultivators, and other

Cobra CSX2149, the 149th Cobra produced, was stored in an Indiana barn for nearly thirty years. The raccoon living in it was angry about his eviction, but he had been a bad tenant, having eaten much of the original leather interior and carpet. *Jim Maxwell*

Once cleaned up from its long nap, the A.C. Cobra began to show promise. At some point, the 21,000-mile car had been painted in a cheap, bronze-metallic color. This is one of the very first rack-and-pinion Cobras, and it is an excellent, unmolested example of the early models. *Jim Maxwell*

farm equipment, Johnny came across an incredible discovery: an authentic A.C. Cobra.

Turns out that the owner, Dr. Bryan Molloy, was a chemist with Lilly Pharmaceuticals and helped develop Prozac. According to his widow, he purchased the Cobra in 1968 or 1969 from an ad in an Indianapolis newspaper. It was already painted brown (over the original white) and he drove it for a couple of years. But his wife eventually convinced him that it was too unsafe to drive, and he parked it in a friend's garage when he lived in the city. When the couple purchased the farm outside of Indianapolis, they moved it to an unheated barn.

The Shelby American World Registry lists CSX2149 as the 149th 289 Cobra manufactured, and it was shipped to Shelby American in July 1963. CSX2149 was manufactured in off-white with a red leather interior, and was ordered with Class "A" accessories, including luggage rack and whitewall tires, for a total price of $5,415.50. The car was then shipped to Ford's district office in

Three years later, CSX2149 has been returned to its original off-white exterior and red leather interior. During its restoration, none of the original parts were replaced, but instead everything was refurbished in order to preserve the car's authenticity. *Tom Cotter*

Davenport, Iowa, for promotional use. Not much more is known of the car until it was purchased by Molloy.

Johnny asked the widow if the car was for sale. He was told that yes it was, but in restored condition it would be worth $80,000 to $90,000. Yet when Johnny offered $30,000, the widow said, "Son, you've bought yourself a car!" Not a bad return on a one-time $4,000 investment. The problem was that Johnny didn't have the money, and he was denied a bank loan, so he borrowed $30,000 from suspicious relatives. He promised to pay them back when he sold the Cobra.

After unloading the accumulated piles of junk that had buried the car for decades, and dragging it out of the barn with a tractor, Johnny discovered that it had been the home of a thirty-pound raccoon who didn't take very kindly to being displaced once the tonneau cover was removed. It seems that Mr. Raccoon had eaten much of the red leather covering the seats and most of the carpet, but the car was generally in good condition.

The car had been driven only 21,000 miles and still retained much of its original equipment, including its low-rise cast-iron intake manifold, the small Y-type exhaust headers, and sparkplug wires. It sported a cheap, metallic bronze paint job over the original off-white.

Johnny brought the car home and word spread quickly that a long-missing Cobra had been discovered. Bids began to come in fast and furiously, from various collectors in the United States and even Canada. Even though the highest bid reached $85,000 (from a Canadian collector), the car was sold to local collector David Doll of Indianapolis for $60,000.

The HiPo 289 engine had not run in twenty-five years, but with a new battery and a splash of fuel, the car was running within fifteen minutes. Doll later installed new Koni shocks and refurbished the car mechanically, but left the exterior and the cosmetics as-found.

Doll had a friend who owned a muscle car museum in Gatlinburg, Tennessee, and he put the Cobra on display there for a while before selling it to Greenville, South Carolina, Harley-Davidson dealer Billy Weaver—who then sold it to Greensboro, North Carolina, Cobra enthusiast Jim Maxwell and buying partner Tom Cotter (yes, *that* Tom Cotter).

Maxwell and Cotter disassembled the car, had it repainted white, and reupholstered the red interior to repair the raccoon's damage. Instead of restoring the car, they refurbished it, and refreshed as many of the removable parts as possible. After spending many years as an ugly duckling, CSX2149 has been transformed once again into a beautiful swan.

The Shelby American Automobile Club (SAAC) says that very few original Cobras are not accounted for, but one wonders how many still reside in barns just beyond view. Fate played a hand in Johnny's find, as within thirty days of his purchase, the barn that had housed CSX2149 for so many years burned to the ground.

Gone but Not Forgotten

BY DAVID B. WILLIAMS

Standing in line at a Terre Haute, Indiana, bank that fall day in 1956, I waited nervously to speak to the teller. I tried to brush off the cobwebs and dirt from my jeans and white T-shirt. My white buckskin shoes were a disaster. I felt out of place, but I waited my turn.

Finally the young teller asked if she could help me. I explained that I wanted to speak to the bank's manager. She replied that he was home sick with a cold and would not be in for the rest of the day. Pressing her, I told her I had to see him and had driven all the way over from Indianapolis. She made a quick call and returned with his name and address.

I drove up to his modest house and nervously knocked on the screen door. Looking through the screen, I could see his wife approaching. She did not smile or invite me inside. She just stated that her husband would be out in a minute. I remember how nervous my stomach had become. What would I say to him? How would he react to me? What if he threw me off the porch or called the police? A number of unpleasant personal disasters were kaleidoscoping in my mind.

Peering once again through the screen, I could see a man of about fifty, short and heavy, begin to take form as he neared the door. Just as he reached for the handle, I said, "Hi, I'm the . . ."

"The car is not for sale!"

"But I would . . ."

"The car is not for sale!"

I was dumbfounded. How did he know what I was about to ask him? As he crossed the porch to the swing, he explained that he knew what I had been up to by the dirt and telltale cobwebs. He sternly added that I had been trespassing and I was not to return to the barn under any circumstances.

I mumbled something about being sorry to have bothered him and started to leave. He called me back, and as I turned, I noticed a slight smile breaking on his previously stern banker face. He invited me to join him on the swing and asked if I wanted to know more about the car.

But first he wanted to know if I had really driven all the way over from Indianapolis and how I had found out about the car. I explained that some friends of mine had been hunting in the area and had spotted what looked like a car covered in a locked barn. They told me it was about five miles east of Terre Haute on the main highway into town. I would see an old abandoned mansion on the left and would find the car in the rear barn.

The banker seemed to be enjoying the story, so on I plunged. I had left that very day in my Model A and had no problem finding the barn. I too looked in the dirty window and through the soft light I had spotted what looked like a covered car.

"How did you get into the barn? I personally locked the sliding door," the banker inquired.

I explained how I had pried the door out and used a rock to wedge the door open, leaving me just enough space to squeeze through. He laughed and said he never thought a person could make it through such a small space.

I then explained how I walked up the center of the barn and could not get over how dusty and dry it was inside. Walking through the curtain of cobwebs, I realized I was in a horse barn with stalls along both sides. Then I came upon the center stall. Someone had removed the center stall's walls, thus making it three stalls wide.

There, sitting sideways, was the huge, canvas-covered rectangle I had spotted through the window. Next to the rectangle, there were four huge steel-spoke wire wheels and tires. This stall was chained and an oversized padlock smiled up defiantly at me. I looked up and noticed how the front of the stall did not reach the top of the barn . . . so up and over I scrambled.

At about this time, the banker's wife appeared with two glasses of iced tea. Still not smiling, she left the drinks on the table and retreated into the house with a slight bang of the screen door. I took a big gulp of the iced tea and blasted forward with the tale.

After scrambling over the stall, I had walked up to the canvas, bent down and took a hold of the bottom of it, and lifted it up to eye level. The sight I beheld will be forever etched in my mind. I saw the longest hood ever known to man. Extracting themselves from the hood were four chrome pipes that quickly disappeared into a gigantic sweeping fender. I looked through the windshield and saw another windshield . . . my god! It was a dual-cowl Duesenberg.

Stepping back and letting the canvas fall, I tripped over the center section of the stall, which was flat on the floor and soon so was I. Was I dreaming? How could this be? I had actually found a Duesie in a barn! A Duesie in a barn! I gathered my wits and went back for another look. I found the dashboard even had an altimeter gauge. In the rear was a large leather trunk. The seats were brown leather and the car was light brown. The driver's door had two initials painted just below the door handle.

The banker then asked how I had tracked him down. I explained that I had carefully covered the car and walked down the road to the next farm to inquire who owned the estate. The farmer was quite informed.

"Old Tom . . . yes . . . it must have been old Tom," the banker laughed.

The banker then told me that I had not been the first to discover the car. Several others had preceded me and had followed much of the same procedure. That is why he had personally locked the barn.

He also said the estate was owned by a wealthy elderly lady. Her husband had purchased the car new. He had passed away many years previously and she had the car placed in the barn. She was now in the local hospital, and when she died the car was to go to her estate.

I could see my visit had run its course. I finished the iced tea and stood to thank the banker for his time and understanding. We shook hands, and I started for my car. After a few steps, I turned back to the house. He was still standing on the top step as if waiting for me to ask one more question. But before I could ask, he said, "Do not go to the hospital and bother her; the car is not for sale."

I sheepishly grinned and promised not to press the matter, and was faithful to my word.

That boy of sixteen is now sixty-five, living in California, and still looking in barns and open garages, still running down leads, and still in love with the chase of old cars. When I hear a barn story, it's hard to resist topping it with the Duesie. I often wonder what happened to it. Who has it? Is it hanging out in Pebble Beach or resting in a private collection?

Do you know the ending for my story? Do you know who got the Duesie in the horse barn on the east side of Terre Haute, Indiana? I would like to know, because in my mind's eye that car will certainly never be forgotten.

The Faucet Fixing Adventure

BY GEORGE GEREG

This is my true cars-in-a-barn story of how I found my 1938 Pontiac woody and 1950 Chevrolet pickup truck. The year was 1978. My father had been buying rhubarb from a local eighty-three-year-old farmer in nearby Brookfield for many years. One day the farmer asked my father if he knew anyone who could repair his faucet. My father mentioned that I could repair it for a fair price. The farmer was interested. When my father told me about the job, I asked him if the farmer had any old cars in the barn, but my father didn't know.

A few days later, I ventured out to the barn (four miles from my house) and met with the farmer. I quickly noticed that the bathroom

After doing some plumbing repairs on an old man's house, George Gereg was given the opportunity to buy this 1938 Pontiac woody. He didn't take any "as-is" photos when he removed it from the barn, but he brought it back for some photos post-restoration. *George Gereg*

fixtures were from the early 1920s. So as I fixed the faucet, I struck up a conversation with the farmer and asked him if he had any old cars in the barn that he would be willing to sell.

He told me he had a '38 Pontiac station wagon and was offered $550 for it many years ago. I asked him if I could see it. He agreed and brought me to a corner of the barn where the windows were covered with cardboard to keep curious eyes out. He quickly opened the barn door and said "Get in quick sonny. A lot of people would like to have this car." I knew after looking at the car what he meant. The car was a "woody." It had Connecticut plates last registered in 1967 and it was a complete car that could be easily restored. I told the farmer that I'd like to buy the car.

But he indicated that he had some "kin" who wanted it. I told him maybe I could give him a better price and to please keep me in mind, but I had pretty much given up hope when I heard about the "kin." A month later, the farmer called me and asked if I was still interested in buying the car. I answered by asking when I could pick it up. He sold it to me for $600 and then handed me back $50 saying, "It needs some new tires." The farmer told me his "kin" didn't invite him to a wedding, so he decided to sell the car to me.

The farmer and I subsequently became good friends, and I often stopped by to visit with him and his dog. Over the years, I continued to restore the car to the original specifications and finished it in 1981. Unfortunately, the farmer didn't live long enough to see the car finished.

Since the farmer didn't have any family in the area, the bank asked me if I could watch the house and barn until the estate was settled. I agreed. I then learned that the contents of the barn were up for bid. The only stipulation was that the barn's contents had to be removed in two months. The relatives didn't want to clean the barn, so I agreed to the amount of $2,500 set by the bank to handle the estate. It was a big job, though. The farmer had saved everything.

The best perk was that the barn included a 1950 Chevy one-ton pickup truck with a hydraulic dump body that had only 37,000 miles on it. But I didn't know where the ignition key was. Luckily, when I felt under the dash, there it was! The truck just needed a little tow truck pull from the barn and it started right up. My father drove it home. We then used it to help clean out the barn. I worked on the truck for five years and finished restoring it in 1987.

Cleaning the barn turned out to be a lot of fun, as I got to discover a whole new set of "treasures." I didn't even have to advertise to get rid of them all. I had dealers stopping in and buying. I even sold the outhouse in the backyard. Toward the end of the two-month's time, I had a big tag sale and got all of my money back and then some.

Overall, 10 tons of scrap metal were removed from the back part outside of the barn. As it was moved, the rain revealed just a bit more metal that still lay hidden. Up until that point, I was missing the crankhole cover from the '38 woody, and I had never even seen what one looked like. Yet when I was walking behind the barn where the 10 tons of metal had been, I saw a broken lower radiator emblem from a '38 Pontiac in the mud. Right near it were two crankhole covers in very good condition. I put the puzzle together and realized that this was just what I needed! I consider this a miracle that the rain uncovered. It is amazing that these metal pieces were not broken or severely pitted.

After I finished the restoration, I drove my '38 Pontiac woody back to the barn to take some final pictures of it in front of its long-time home. I am glad I did, since the barn fell down and was removed a few years ago. All I can say is that I was in the right place at the right time. This was a once in a lifetime experience that I will never forget.

Found and Lost and Found Again!

On July 17, 1953, the National Hot Rod Association founder and then-editor of *Hot Rod Magazine*, Wally Parks, sat down to type up a letter responding to Mr. Bud Neumeister, who had proposed to do a series of stories on constructing a "conservative" hot rod.

"We definitely want your step-by-step description of construction," wrote Parks, who also asked for an exclusive for his magazine. "We can establish payment rates for your material, which I am sure will be satisfactory to you."

To build the hot rod, Neumeister needed a base car and he searched long and hard to find it. Finally he saw what he needed in Pueblo, Colorado. "It might have looked a bit neglected to the average passerby, but to me that Model A roadster parked in the alley meant the end to a long, long search," he wrote in his May 1954 article. When he asked the price, the seller said "I'll take a hundred for it." Done deal.

Neumeister then set about disassembling and modifying the car while documenting the process for his *Hot Rod* articles, both as a

Above and opposite: From the Neumeister family photo album, here are images of the '28 Model A Ford being built in the family's driveway in Colorado in 1953. That's Bud's daughter, Cheryl, checking out the front wheels at the far right. *Bud Neumeister/Roger Morrison*

writer and photographer. "I'd made up my mind that what I wanted was a car that looked absolutely stock on the out-side, but was actually a fast, dependable, well handling machine," he wrote. He then proceeded to rebuild the Model A with a 1939 Ford gearbox, pedal assembly and hydraulic brakes, 1941 Ford front spindles, and 1937 Chevrolet tailpipes. The concluding chapter appeared in the June 1954 issue, and it covered the interior installation, engine buildup, and assembly.

For his two-part story, Neumeister received the handsome fee of $300 from Parks, along with a sincere letter of appreciation for delivering such a fine prod-uct. Neumeister kept the hot rod, investing three years and more than $2,500 in the car, which he used throughout the 1950s in auto rallies and hill-climbs, including Pikes Peak. Eventually he was bitten by the sports car bug and sold the Model A to buy a Porsche, probably around 1960. "I knew it was a mistake, but I sold it anyway," he said in a magazine story years later.

However, the hot rod that Neumeister invested so much

Bud Neumeister wrote a two-part series for *Hot Rod Magazine* on the construction of his roadster (note upper right). *Roger Morrison*

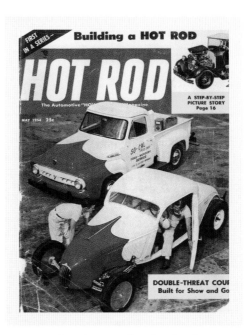

in was not gone forever. Thirty years and ten owners later, the car ended up in a storage building at a salvage yard. Neumeister went to the yard on another project and wandered into the building. There, under a tarp, was his old Model A, and it was for sale. He didn't let it go again. As he told *Hot Rod* in April 1997, "it's like getting a family member back. There are a lot of memories in this car."

Above and opposite: Again from the family album, Neumeister shows off his completed hot rod in 1957. He competed with the car in sports car events, such as road rallies and hillclimbs—unusual for a hot rod. *Bud Neumeister/Roger Morrison*

In 2002, Neumeister was diagnosed with multiple types of cancer. He decided that the best use for his beloved roadster was to sell it at the Goodguys show that year and use the money to help fund his grandson's college education. Unfortunately, the people who expressed interest in the car did not have the same appreciation for it that Neumeister did. They wanted to put a Chevy engine in it and add new wheels, which would have changed the character of the car and what it stood for. Instead, he took the car home in frustration.

Collector Roger Morrison heard about the rediscovered hot rod and committed by phone to buy the car. "I enjoy cars with documented history," he says. Because Neumeister's health was rapidly deteriorating, Morrison made it his goal to have the car restored in time for the 2003 Goodguys show in Colorado Springs. He did finish it in time and the car received the "Gazette Pick" award. Neumeister even rode with Morrison in the car to receive the trophy.

Freshly restored, the Model A was recognized at the Colorado Springs Goodguys show in 2003. *Roger Morrison*

This accomplished, Morrison readied the car for the Grand National Roadster Show. Neumeister and his daughter, Cheryl, drove from Pueblo to Los Angeles to attend the show, and had a terrific time. It was even more terrific when the car won its class.

Neumeister was also able to meet Wally Parks, for whom he had written about the same car a half-century earlier. Afterwards, Neumeister's daughter wrote a letter to Morrison, thanking him for becoming the caretaker of her father's beloved hot rod. "You have been responsible for providing one of the high points in my dad's life, and I can't find the words to express how grateful I am for that," she said. "To see him as happy and thrilled as I did when he saw the car sitting there in all its splendor, and then finally meeting Wally Parks, will stay with me all my life."

Today, Neumeister is in frail health, but still has cars in his blood. He stays involved in his passion by helping on his son's Formula V racing program.

CHAPTER TWO

Fetching
the Lotus

BY PETER EGAN
COURTESY OF *ROAD & TRACK*,
PUBLISHED IN JUNE 2004

"I wouldn't even sell a car to someone who had a trailer that old and dirty," Barb said on a late-night visit to my workshop. I extracted my head from a fender well and stood up with my hands held slightly outward, like a statue of a welcoming saint—a saint with big gobs of fresh wheel-bearing grease in the palms of his hands—and appraised the trailer.

"Well," I said defensively, "you haven't seen the car we're picking up in New Jersey. It's been in a barn for the past twenty years, just like this trailer. I think the car owner will understand."

In truth, I was a little unsettled by Barb's observation, as I'd already spent three days getting the trailer ready for its upcoming trip. I'd borrowed this rig from Chris Beebe, my old friend and neighbor, who warned me it was buried under a pile of sheet metal in his old tobacco barn and frozen to the ground on two flat tires.

So, I'd gone over one frigid winter morning, dressed in my best insulated Carhartt coveralls and Elmer Fudd cap, toting a compressed air tank and a scissor jack. A few hours later, with no more suffering than you'd normally experience having a molar extracted, I had the trailer wrenched from the frozen earth and sitting in the farmyard on two semi-inflated old tires.

I stood and looked at the trailer; I was out of breath and completely exhausted. Blood dripped into the snow from where I'd cut my hands on the rough edges of the trailer fenders.

"The things we do for cars," I said, my steaming words carried away by the subzero Wisconsin wind.

Then I deftly smashed my left hand with a breaker bar while installing a ball hitch on my blue Ford Econoline van and hopped around on one foot to facilitate cursing before hooking up the trailer. A local tire shop installed two of the best tires money could buy for $36 each, after which I towed the trailer home to install new wheel bearings. I was just finishing the job when Barb made her offhand comment about the trailer.

She was right. It did look a little rough.

I had to use it, though. It was a matter of history and symbolic importance. Chris Beebe had used this trailer to haul his newly purchased Lotus Super Seven race car back from California in 1971. It was originally a small U-Haul flatbed, but Chris had spent several days with an arc welder, artfully lightening, gusseting, and reengineering the trailer to fit his Lotus Seven for the trip home.

The results were structurally sound rather than elegant. The trailer was light, low, and minimal in design; it was no bigger or smaller than it had to be to haul a Super Seven. It was the Lotus of trailers.

Chris used it for years to haul his very competitive car to SCCA races, and he even took it to the Runoffs in Road Atlanta one year. The old thing had a proud history.

Now it was out of retirement, and about to go all the way to the

Egan inspects his newly purchased Lotus Elan in the New Jersey barn that cold winter morning. *Chris Beebe*

East Coast to pick up another Lotus of similar dimensions and weight—an Elan this time.

Yes, after owning three Lotus Sevens in my life, I was finally stepping up one generation in the Lotus family and buying an Elan. (By the time I'm ninety years old, I'll probably have a Europa.)

This whole deal came about because I shot my mouth off in print a few months ago (or shot my word processor off . . . whatever) in a column in which I confessed that a Lotus Elan was on my short list of favorite cars.

Lo and behold, I got an email from a man named Tom Cochran in rural New Jersey. He was the original owner of a 1964 Series 1 Elan, bought new from Cox & Pulver on Madison Avenue in downtown Manhattan. He'd driven it regularly for nearly twenty years, taking frequent ski trips to Vermont, and had then put it up on blocks in his barn in 1983. The fuel lines were leaking, he said. So were the rear brake lines. The replaceable subframe was cracked and rusty, and the car would need a complete restoration.

Naturally, I called Tom to get more details about the Lotus, and to find out how much he wanted for it. The price he named was just low enough to make the car irresistible to an excitable person such as myself, while leaving financial room for a decent restoration, at my usual free labor rate.

He sent me photos of the Lotus. It was faded red with a black top—a very early six-taillight model—sitting in all its dusty glory, covered with tiny mouse droppings, and resting on blocks in the corner of an old barn made of huge timbers. In other words, it was perfect.

"I'll be out next Wednesday," I told him.

Chris not only volunteered to come along, but also welded new fenders on the trailer before we left, "just so we'll be objects of admiration virtually wherever we go."

Early on Tuesday morning, we headed out for New Jersey. With our new wheel bearings whirling like greasy, trouble-free dervishes through downtown Chicago, we took I-80 across Indiana and Ohio and made it into eastern Pennsylvania the first night, after a detour around a horrendous chain-reaction pileup caused by blinding snow squalls near Lock Haven. Thirty semis and twenty cars were wrecked.

We crossed the Delaware River and got to Tom's place at noon the next day. He and his wife, Tabby, have a lovely old Colonial country home built in 1750, on fifteen acres of hilly, wooded land. It is believed, Tom told us, that George Washington and his troops camped on this property on their way to Trenton during the Revolutionary War.

"And two hundred years later, there's a British car in the barn," Chris noted.

"Redcoats' revenge," I said. "Last tag."

True to the photos, the car sat in the corner of an old green barn, with beams of light falling Caravaggio-like on its subtle and dusty curves from a nearby window. Chris (who owns two Lotus Elans himself) helped me look it over. It was as represented—a rusty subframe in need of replacement; minor body damage in front of the right door, properly repaired; paint with lots of patina. It was an essentially unmolested car with all its original parts. We bolted on the wheels, lowered the car from the blocks, and loaded the Elan on the Lotus of car trailers. After it was tied down, I noticed that Tom had grown very quiet and still.

I glanced over and saw a look of great sadness in his eyes, possibly mixed with remorse.

"Are you sure you want to do this?" I asked.

"We have a lot of history with this car," he said. "I met my wife when I first had the Lotus. We took ski trips together. I have pictures of our kids sitting in it when they were little. But it needs to be restored and I'll never get around to it. The car needs a good home."

Tabby invited us in for lunch with their daughter Oakley, and I learned that Tom had been a *Road & Track* reader since 1949. He had owned three Morgans, including a Super Sport, and he had a new Lotus Elise on order. He'd driven the Elan to Watkins Glen and to sports-car races all over the East Coast.

Tabby said, "I've got to show you a Christmas stocking I made for Tom in the mid-60s."

She left and returned with a big red felt stocking that had a hand-stitched profile of an Elan on one side and a skier on the other. One side said LOTUS in large letters and the other side said SKIING.

"His two favorite things," she told me.

Now it was my time to grow quiet and still.

After lunch we said goodbye and headed for Wisconsin. As we pulled out of the driveway and waved, Chris said, "What a wonderful family." I nodded. "Nice people, a beautiful setting, and a handsome old car in an ancient barn," he continued. "It's like something out of a dream." I had the feeling we were driving away with a family heirloom, rather than just another unwanted project car.

We made it home in a day and a half. I dropped Chris off at his house, unloaded the car in the snowy darkness, rolled it into my workshop, turned on the lights, and cranked up the heat.

I stayed up until three in the morning, puttering around with the car, cleaning, vacuuming mouse nests from under the seats, and just sitting back to look at it. I finally went to bed, but couldn't sleep. I was filled with too much adrenaline. So I got up early, made some coffee, and went back out to the workshop to gaze upon the Elan. A light snow was falling on the trailer outside.

I sat there for a while and tried to think if anything could be more fun on a dark and wintry week than going on a road trip and bringing a nice old car home to restore.

I couldn't think of anything, even after a second cup of coffee. Retrieving an old car, of course, is always the best and easiest part. The hard work of restoration comes later, like your Visa bill after a night on the town. I believe this is called deficit living.

CHAPTER THREE

Rare Birds

A Ford Built for Royalty

The Vanderbilts: America's royal family at the turn of the last century. Builders of railroads and industry like this country had never seen before. Wealthy beyond imagination.

The Vanderbilts also had a thing for cars. William K. Vanderbilt was a promoter of auto races in the early 1900s. In fact, he hosted the Vanderbilt Cup races on Long Island's Motor Parkway, the family's private toll road.

The Vanderbilts had the finest cars at their disposal, not only in the United States, but around the world. No matter what kind of car, be it a Packard or Duesenberg or Lincoln, they were nearly always painted maroon and black. This is the story of one of those maroon and black cars, but a much more lowly brand than the family's usual great marques.

The story goes that the Vanderbilt's chauffeurs took great pride in maintaining the family's limousines. When they became attached to a particular body, the family often used that body again, although with a new chassis and drivetrain. So when it was time to retire a 1929 Renault town car, the body was simply moved to a similarly sized 1935 Ford chassis.

A lot of modification was needed to adapt the aluminum body, which had been crafted by the Kellner Body Company in France, to the Dearborn, Michigan–produced Ford. For instance, the Ford rear fenders, which were steel, were widened because the Renault body was narrower than a standard Ford body.

So how did this car, once owned by one of the richest families in the world, fall from grace and wind up in a barn on eastern Long Island?

Jim Mooney first saw this rare, one-off car built for the Vanderbilt family sitting dusty and forgotten in a carriage house on eastern Long Island in 1971. It is unique in that its French-built 1929 Kellner body is mounted on a 1935 Ford modified chassis. *Jim Mooney*

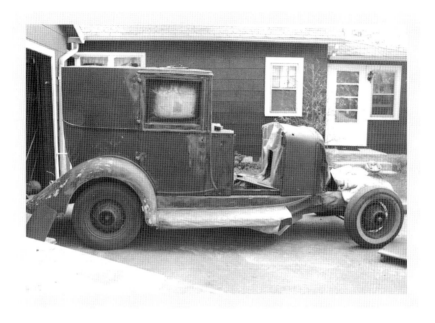

When he got the restoration underway in 1972, Mooney discovered that much of the body—the front and rear fenders, running boards, and cowl—had been extensively modified in order to mate the exotic aluminum body to the Ford. *Jim Mooney*

That's what eventual owner Jim Mooney of Lake Ronkonkoma, New York, tried to find out.

After he purchased the town car, Mooney traveled to Rhode Island—where the Vanderbilts had many ocean-front estates—in hopes of learning more about his curious purchase. It seems that the '35 Ford town car was driven to the Newport, Rhode Island, Ford dealership and traded in on a brand-new '51 Ford. The trade-in value was $600.

A later owner used the car as collateral to buy a liquor store, but he went bankrupt and lost the Ford. Then a man from Westhampton, New York, bought the car at auction and stuck it in his barn on eastern Long Island.

In November 1970, Mooney's friend Ben Dobrey talked with him about an odd '35 Ford that he had just spotted during his job as a power company meter reader. Dobrey sketched the car on a napkin

The Cobra in the Barn's author and his new wife, Pat, celebrate on the way to their wedding reception on August 22, 1976, in Jim Mooney's town car. Pat's grandfather, Joseph Santantonio, poses as the chauffeur. *Jim Mooney*

for Mooney. "Impossible," said Mooney, who was an avid Ford collector and restorer. Two months later, in January, the two were parts hunting in the area where the '35 Ford was located, so they decided to take a look at the car.

The car was being stored in the carriage house of a posh, winter-deserted estate. A caretaker and his wife did live there, and it took some fancy talking by Mooney to gain permission to inspect the car. "It took us about an hour to convince the couple that we weren't going to burglarize the joint," Mooney says. Eventually, the care-taker allowed them to go into the barn to look at the car. They were not permitted to touch the car or open any of the doors, though. Mooney, who is a professional photographer, was allowed to take photos of the car as long as he agreed not to mention the location of the car to anyone. The caretaker said that the car's owner was spend-ing the winter in Europe.

Six months later, in June, Mooney made another attempt to meet with the owner of the car, figuring he might spend summers at his estate. The man was home, and he agreed to sell the Ford for the same price he paid for it at an auction seven years earlier. Mooney promptly paid the man and hooked the Ford to the tow bar on his Bronco. On the tow home, he soon realized, based on all the attention and stares he received from other motorists on the road, that he now owned a very special car.

Mooney immediately started to disassemble the Ford in order to begin its restoration. In the process, he discovered some fascinating items. One was a one-way intercom, which passengers in the back seat would use to communicate to the chauffeur. The chauffeur, however, had no means to respond. The Kellner body was made entirely of aluminum, with the exception of the four fenders and the hood, which were modified steel Ford parts. The passenger compartment was insulated with genuine horsehair, and the rear seats were upholstered in mohair.

Since the chassis only had 27,000 miles on it, the Ford parts, such as the running boards and gauges, were in nearly perfect condition.

The restoration was challenging, since so many parts that appeared to be standard Ford items had in fact been altered to fit the Renault body. The hood, for example, is much shorter than a standard 1935 Ford hood. Also, the Kellner body was difficult to work on because there were so many wood shims that had been installed so the body would sit squarely on the frame and the doors would operate properly.

Mooney did his best to match the original Vanderbilt maroon, which was difficult because all the maroon samples that were similar were metallic and the original paint was matte. Ultimately, with the help of his artist brother Jerry, Mooney was able to create a color close to the proper shade.

He completed the restoration in less than one year, and Mooney's one-of-a-kind town car was the hit of the old Ford show circuit. He once drove the town car to Detroit for an Early Ford V-8

Club national convention, and a local television news broadcaster did a story about the interesting car while sitting in the chauffeur's compartment with a proper chauffeur's cap on.

Owning such a unique car inspired Mooney to start a business—Vintage Livery Service, which also featured his '36 Ford stretched airport limo. Mooney's cars added a touch of automotive elegance to weddings and other formal affairs around Long Island.

Mooney sold the rare '35 Ford town car in 1980, and wonders where it might be today. He believes it's in Texas. He wonders if it might be sitting in an old barn on an empty estate and, of course, if it might be for sale.

Another Mooney barn find to complement the town car: a stretched 1936 Ford airport limousine, which Mooney found in 1974. Some guys have all the luck. *Jim Mooney*

The Cape Cod Healey

BY KRIS PALMER

Donald Paye knew a little about Austin-Healeys. He loved the styling and had owned a few Healey 100s. He even had some spare engines and gearboxes lying around. He also had a friend who had been into Healeys for many years and had a number of them, including a rare 100S (S for Sebring), a special version with aluminum panels and a modified engine and disc brakes built for racing.

While at a Healey meet on Cape Cod in 1976, Paye began thumbing through another attendee's copy of *Hemmings Motor News*. A small ad caught his eye: Austin-Healey, excellent body, no motor, no transmission. Since he had a spare engine and transmission, Paye decided to give the seller a call, thinking he might be able to make a runner and have some fun.

As he questioned the seller about the car, the man said he'd scratched the paint years ago and it never rusted. This made the seller think the body might be aluminum, and suddenly Paye's mind shifted into a new gear. Only early and special cars had all-aluminum bodies.

Paye quickly told the seller he would come to look at it. He brought a trailer and his Healey-expert friend to see it in Saugerties, New York. They also brought some magnets to ensure the body was aluminum, as the seller believed.

As eager as he was to see the car, Paye hesitated as they approached the barn. It was falling down around the car. It looked like a strong wind or a few extra pigeons on the roof would cause the whole thing to collapse, leaving the car a total write-off.

Carefully, they inspected it and found the seller's claims were genuine. What looked like aluminum was indeed; the magnets fell to the floor. While the engine and transmission had gone to another car, the rest was largely complete. Paye and his friend noticed that some of the pieces, such as latches and trim, were nonstandard. Someone had painted the car, including racing stripes, but the body was sound. Paye struck a deal and they loaded the car onto a trailer for the trip back to Massachusetts.

On the way to Paye's house, they stopped at his friend's to check the chassis number against a reference book. What they found was puzzling. The production numbers in the book started at a higher number than this car's chassis I.D. Was it a pre-production car? The only way to be sure was to take his question directly to the source: Paye wrote to Healey Automobile Consultants in Warwick, England, a successor company to the Donald Healey Motor Corporation.

A few weeks later, Paye received a letter from the United Kingdom. The writer was none other than Geoffrey Healey, son of Donald (the creator of the Austin-Healey automobile). His first words confirmed Paye's suspicions:

"You are indeed a lucky man! Your car is one of the first four 'pre-production cars' built at Warwick for the U.S.A.," he said.

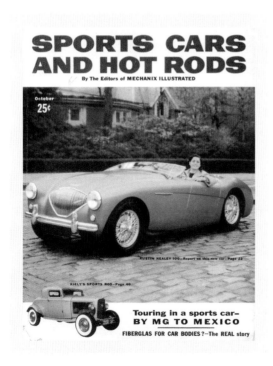

When Donald Paye's Austin-Healey was new, it received a lot of media attention in the United States. Here Paye's car appears on the cover of *Sports Cars and Hot Rods* magazine in October 1953. *Donald Paye Collection*

Donald Healey toured the United States in Paye's car in 1953 while promoting the brand and trying to set up dealerships.

The four cars, registered AHX1, AHX2, AHX3, and AHX4, were shipped aboard the *Queen Elizabeth* or *Queen Mary* out of Southampton, England, in February or March 1953. Paye's car was assigned registration number AHX3, although it was the second car produced as identified by its chassis serial number. The first car produced, registered AHX4, has not been rediscovered, making Paye's car the oldest Austin-Healey in the world.

Geoffrey Healey told Paye his car was originally painted Healey Ice Blue, and Paye found this color under the "new" paint job. Healey also mentioned that the engine would have been the same as the 100, though it originally may have had some handmade parts. Paye's early 2.6-liter Austin A90 sedan engine and three-speed overdrive gearbox were therefore basically correct for the car. Note that the gearbox was actually a four-speed, but the first gear was too low in Healey's mind, so he blanked it off and added overdrive.

Number 2, as Paye calls it, has several distinct features that separate it from other early 100s. These include a peaked grille with chrome-plated, extruded brass trim ring with vertical slats set in lead; handmade 100 flash emblem; one-piece front shroud; stock chrome wire wheels; different door, hood, and trunk latches; different side screen sockets; one-piece plexiglass side screens; and extruded-brass cockpit surround.

Although the car isn't quite finished, Paye is completing proper restoration efforts, including replacing one steel fender that had been substituted for the aluminum original likely because of accident damage. Paye found a metalsmith in Canada who builds race car bodies, and the metalsmith was able to reproduce the proper fender shape in aluminum. The body tub also was stripped of paint, rust, and oil, the minor body and chassis damage repaired, and the exterior restored to the proper, original color.

Since the car surfaced in 1976, many of the men involved in its early development have been reunited with it, including Donald

Restored to its original color and condition, Paye's Healey is the earliest known example in existence.
Donald Paye

Healey, Gerry Coker, John Wheatley, and Roger Menadue. Menadue was Donald Healey's right-hand man and he built the early cars. Paye had the honor of hosting Menadue at his home when the former Healey builder came out to Cape Cod to see a Nash-Healey race car. He had called the Healey Club inquiring where to stay, and the club referred him to Paye.

For Paye, Menadue's visit has been the highlight of owning Number 2. The meeting, and the things he learned during it, had an air of destiny. Menadue remembered building the car and explained to Paye how and why some of the unique items were made as they were. He verified things, knew about the unique trim, and mentioned various changes as production started.

Paye was also impressed by Menadue's modesty. Here in the United States, we may think of a car builder as someone like Lee Iacocca, a wealthy and prominent public figure. The men behind the Austin-Healey were not men of great wealth. They built cars for the love of automobiles. Menadue told Paye he never owned a car or a telephone, though he had use of both.

Donald Healey, who was also reunited with Number 2, initially didn't want to show the Healey 100 (named for its 100 horsepower and claimed ability to reach 100 miles per hour) at the 1952 Earls Court Motor Show. He initially didn't like the prototype's nose design, and asked that if the car had to be shown, it would be positioned with the front end toward a wall or pole. Soon after the design was redone, and the car became a huge hit—so much so that the president of Austin approached Healey about it. Healey had a deal for Austin engines, but planned to build the car himself. But Austin's president convinced Healey that his operation was too small to meet demand. He proposed a joint venture, and Austin-Healey was formed. They reportedly developed the famous Austin-Healey logo within days of this encounter.

Menadue's visit brought the "Number 2" adventure full circle. This car, built in the earliest days of the company and used to promote it in the United States, had slipped from public view, lost its running gear, and ended up in a barn disguised under nonstandard paint. Only intuition and lucky timing saved the car from being destroyed by the very barn that had provided it refuge. Its reprise brought excitement and fond memories not only to Paye, but to the men who had created the car two decades before.

Paye has always loved Austin-Healey, and Number 2 has linked him to that company's history. Geoffrey Healey got it right: Paye is indeed a lucky man.

An MG to Remember

BY KRIS PALMER

Malcolm Appleton has a small collection of older MGs, including two pre-war examples. He loves the simple, robust cars built in this era, and he was always looking for a special car—something rare, something unique. It came to him the way these things often do, in a way he never expected.

At a cocktail party in Stowe, Vermont, Appleton struck up a conversation with a man from Montreal. The man was not obsessed with cars, but because Appleton was, the conversation eventually went in that direction. As Appleton described his MGs, the man listened with some interest, then they parted ways. Appleton then left to attend to some business in England.

When he returned, among his many messages was one from a man whose name he didn't recognize. He called and it turned out to be the Canadian he'd met in Stowe. This man liked to take walks and had

Here's the first rule of barn finding: let people know you like old cars. Malcolm Appleton met a Canadian at a Stowe, Vermont, cocktail party and mentioned he liked old MGs. Soon, the man called Appleton and said he saw this unusual six-cylinder MG in a barn near his home. *Malcolm Appleton*

an eye for old cars tucked away. He'd spotted something interesting in a barn-garage. It was an MG, and its owner was interested in selling.

There are a lot of stored MGs, and most are nothing unusual.

"What kind of MG?" Appleton asked.

"It's a six-cylinder," the man responded. "A Magna with a 'boat-tail.'"

When he heard that, Appleton just about fell off his chair. He phoned the seller immediately.

The car's owner was a Scot who had come to Canada to teach. He hadn't found the time to restore the car and it appeared he wasn't going to. It was time to part with it, but he wasn't going to sell the unique British tourer to just anyone. He told Appleton he wanted to meet him.

Appleton departed promptly for Montreal. When he got there, what he saw would not have impressed everyone. "It was a sad and sorry-looking piece of machinery," he says. It was up on blocks, where it had been put away twenty-five years earlier. It showed signs of restoration and re-restoration. But Appleton did not see the car with layman's eyes. He knew MGs well, and he was aware that this was a rare car. The boat-tail coachwork with "dickey seat" was one of few Stiles bodies mated to an MG Magna. Most critical, the car was complete, right down to the original wheels.

The owner was impressed with Appleton's knowledge and love of MGs. He had already turned down several prospective buyers. They were resellers or people looking for a project to "fix up." When Appleton said he planned a full restoration, they struck a deal and the car left Canada for its new home in Vermont.

Auto restoration is a bit like archaeology in that you have to dig down to learn what's really there. The overhead-cam six-cylinder engine was original and complete, but the head was cracked. Luckily, Appleton's engine builder found that the motor had been well looked after and it would be a good powerplant once the head was welded up. The radiator needed a new core, but that was to be expected. At least the car included the original grille shell.

This is Appleton's rare 1931 MG Magna F1, just as it left the barn near Montreal. The car had been restored and re-restored, but sat on blocks for twenty-five years until Appleton discovered it. *Malcolm Appleton*

The seats had been recovered in black, but the person who did it left the original covers beneath. Though they were unsalvageable, they provided Appleton with exact specifications for new ones. The original seat innards likewise allowed for exact replication in the finished car, which will reuse some of the original seat springs and feature the correct seat padding and contours.

In his research, Appleton tracked down an original Stiles sales brochure. Stiles was a company, like many of the period, that offered custom bodies for cars produced by auto manufacturers. These special bodies had features and color schemes unavailable in the production models. One color scheme described in the Stiles brochure featured a cream-colored chassis with a sky-blue metallic body. Separating the two components, Appleton discovered both colors on his Magna, not only identifying the proper color scheme, but allowing for a proper match of the original paint.

Eventually, other interesting features came to light. Stiles had offered a side-mounted spare tire during this period, which this car

Appleton's MG was imported to Canada sometime in the 1950s, where it was used for ice racing. This photograph of the same car shows notes on the bottom that only 1,250 were manufactured, but actually, the number of MGs that had a Stiles body, like Appleton's does, was only 30. *Malcolm Appleton*

1932 F   OUT OF 1250 MADE
1271 CC 6 CYL OHC

did not appear to have. In redoing the car, however, Appleton discovered mounting holes on the side of the car, as well as some of the bracketry. For a self-described restoration fanatic, this meant that the finished car would also wear a side-mounted spare.

The Stiles Magna also has an interesting windshield. Drophead cars of the period, including MGs, often had fold-down windshields for a real open, wind-in-the-hair feel. The Stiles Magna's windshield is hinged not only at the bottom, to fold down, but also along the top. This allows occupants to push the bottom of the windshield outward for a rush of fresh air even when the car's soft top is raised.

The body's aluminum and wood componentry were all there, and the wood—remarkably—was all reusable. Much of the aluminum had corroded beyond rescue, however. What wouldn't go on the car could at least provide a precise template for new pieces. After a determined search, Appleton found a man in New Hampshire able to make exact reproductions of the needed parts.

A few original pieces were missing—such as the original knock-off wheel spinners—but Appleton tracked down a set in England for the finished car.

Stiles produced only thirty custom-bodied Magnas. Fewer than eight survive. Of these, Appleton's is the only one in the United States and the most complete and original example in the world. Owners of other cars have contacted him, and even flown to Vermont from Europe, to see Appleton's Magna for perspective in restoring their own.

Appleton has the original bill of sale from MG, showing that the Magna chassis was to be mated with a Stiles body. A doctor from Harley Street in London had made the purchase. Appleton has even tracked down and spoken to the original owner's sister. He also discovered that the car went to Canada in the 1950s or 1960s, where it was at one time used for ice racing. The rare Magna then took up residency in a Canadian-Scotsman's barn-garage, and began its quarter-century wait for a walker with a keen eye.

Asked what he plans to do with the car, Appleton says, "Keep it, definitely." He will take it to shows, enjoy it on the roads, and then pass it on to his children.

With the restoration completed, Appleton races his MG in a re-enactment of the Round-the-Houses race in Alexandria Bay in 1999. The race is sponsored by the *New England MGT Register. Malcolm Appleton*

A Ferrari Behind the Barn

Bill Locke thought he had uncovered the automotive equivalent of King Tut's tomb back in 1984. That's the day his Corvette buddy from Bradenton, Florida, called to say, "You wouldn't believe what I just saw sitting behind a sports car repair shop!"

Locke has two automotive interests: Corvettes and Ferraris. Since the mid-1970s, the retired banking executive has owned at least one of each and to this day is the event director at the Bloomington Gold Corvette Hall of Fame. But he has always been smitten with the Ferrari mystique. He purchased his first Ferrari in 1975, a 330 GTC, but has owned a number of others—including a 365 GTB 4, a Daytona, two Dino Spyders, a 512 BB, an early '76 fiberglass 308, and both a short- and long-nose 275 GTB. Like all diehard car collectors, Locke was always looking for the next project.

What Bill Locke had hoped was a Ferrari California Spyder (because he saw covered headlights on the car) was actually a 250 Cabriolet. Nobody could say how or why the car came to be stored outside a foreign car repair shop in Florida. *Bill Locke*

One classy rat chose to take up residence inside the Ferrari's glove box. Evidence of its home was found throughout the interior, trunk, and engine compartment of this once-proud car. Wonder what Enzo would have thought . . . *Bill Locke*

So when his friend called to tell him of the Ferrari he had discovered, Locke was all ears.

"Is it an open or closed car?" he asked.

"It's an open car," his buddy said.

"Does it have covered or exposed headlights?" Locke further asked.

His friend wasn't sure, so he said he'd go back and check.

"I just knew in my heart that it was a California Spyder, and only wondered if it was a short or long wheelbase, and whether it was one of the aluminum racing models," Locke says.

"I didn't care what condition it was in, I just had to have it."

His friend called again to tell him it had enclosed headlights. Locke's heart nearly stopped. "One more question: does it have vent windows?" he asked as he held his breath. "Yes it does," his friend responded.

Locke's heart sank. With vent windows, the car couldn't be a California Spyder, which restored could fetch $2.5 million.

It was probably a GT Series II, but a car still worth following up on.

Locke says the price was right, so he negotiated the car's purchase without ever seeing it. He then hooked up his trailer to his truck and went to retrieve his new acquisition.

Locke's hunch was correct. The car turned out to be a 1961 Ferrari 250 GT Series II Cabriolet—one of only 202 built—that had been mildly modified by a previous owner to resemble a California. Even though this was one of the few 250 GT Cabriolets actually equipped with covered headlights, the rear fascia had been redesigned by a previous owner, resulting in the added spoiler and the altered taillights.

"Any twelve-cylinder convertible Ferrari has a special place in automotive history," Locke says.

But the car was in rough shape when he found it. It had been parked behind the foreign car repair shop for a number of years. "The car was sitting outside with a ripped top and no cover," he says.

And what the critters and Mother Nature didn't destroy, creative bodymen tried to. For some reason, an earlier owner wanted the Ferrari to look like a Fiat, so these awful taillights were added. *Bill Locke*

"I have no idea how long it was sitting, but the car was last titled in 1973, so it could have been a decade."

The actual owner was a land surveyor, but Locke didn't ask too many questions, fearing his enthusiasm would raise a red flag and spoil the sale.

Once he brought the car home, he put it in his garage and never touched it. "I'd walk around it every evening and ask myself, 'What have I gotten myself into?'" he says. The Ferrari's floors and trunk area were full of rust. He also discovered a rat's nest in the glove box and evidence that some critter had made its home in the trunk.

Rebuilding it wasn't going to be cheap, even in 1984. "The mechanical rebuild alone could cost in excess of fifty thousand dollars," Locke says. "Then you've got to buy the Connolly leather, the Wilton carpet, chrome, rubber, and electrical systems; even at just forty dollars per hour, at three thousand hours, that's one-hundred-twenty thousand dollars in labor alone.

"At the time, we owned three very nice Ferraris, so my wife Pat thought someone else should own this project," he says. So Locke sold the Ferrari six months after purchasing it, to a friend who was a fellow Ferrari enthusiast. His friend still has that car today, and is finally ready to begin restoration. "I found another Ferrari I wanted more, and sold the first one to produce some cash," Locke says.

He figures the restored Ferrari would be worth about $225,000 to $300,000 in today's market, and even in its rough as-is condition, it would probably bring $125,000, a number far more than he sold the car for twenty years ago.

"I wish that I hadn't sold that car," he says. "I'd love to have it back. But I've noticed that automotive hindsight is always 20/20."

The Ojai Sports Cars

C hris Hilgers lives in Ojai, California, one of those picturesque little spots nestled up in the mountains north of Los Angeles that makes visitors want to sell everything they own and move there. Hilgers runs a grading business in town along with his son. "My business allows me the opportunity to go onto people's properties where others can't go," he says, "and so I always have my eyes open for interesting old cars."

CAR NO. 1, 1965 GRIFFITH SERIES 200

One day Hilgers was riding around his little town and came across a housing tract about five miles from his home. "I came across this driveway filled with cars under rotting blue tarps," he says, "and I had to find out what kind of cars were under those tarps."

So Hilgers did what any old car enthusiast would do—he crept up to the house and took a peek. He thought he'd hit the mother

Soon after dragging the Griffith several blocks from his home, Chris Hilgers and his friends examine the new project. Much to his disappointment, many of the chassis tubes, which were not much thicker than exhaust pipe, had deteriorated because they were bonded into the car's fiberglass body. *Chris Hilgers*

lode: six cars, all of which were interesting. He saw a Sunbeam Tiger, an Aston Martin DB3, a Jaguar E-Type, a Lincoln Continental convertible, and a '56 Chevy. But the car that he was most intrigued with was the Griffith Series 200 sports car.

Many car enthusiasts have a hard time identifying a Griffith. It is based on the British TVR sports car, but with a Ford high-perform-ance V-8 installed. The Griffiths were manufactured on Long Island, New York, by Ford dealer Jack Griffith, whose intention was to grab a little piece of all that money Carroll Shelby was raking in with his A.C. Cobra. Griffith Ford was also a Shelby dealer. In fact, it was the East Coast storage facility for A.C. bodies that awaited shipping to Shelby's Venice, California, facility.

To make the Griffiths, Griffith hired a handful of qualified mechanics, machinists, and fabricators to install HiPo 289 engines into the small fiberglass cars. He also hired Mark Donohue as a test driver. Donohue went on to become a renowned driver and winner in Trans Am, Can Am, Indy, and a multitude of other motorsports categories.

"I was attracted to the car because I'm a high-horsepower nut, and it was unusual," Hilgers says. So he knocked on the door of the home where all the cars were parked, but nobody was home. "But I recognized the name on the door as somebody who worked for another contractor friend of mine, so I called him and he said, 'Sure, I'll sell you the car.'"

Hilgers says that in hindsight he wished he had purchased the Aston Martin, but it and the rest of the cars were significantly more expensive than the Griffith. "Turns out this guy inherited these cars from his dad about seventeen years earlier," Hilgers says. "They were all running at the time. But he just parked them in his driveway, cov-ered them with tarps, and never looked at them again. His driveway was so crowded that he had to park his own car in the street."

So Hilgers had the Griffith, the 108th built, towed to his home, avoiding his friend's suggestion of driving it in "the dip" on the way home. The dip, on Grand Street near his house, is a favorite spot for

The former barn find shows off its new front suspension and engine. Hilgers decided to rebuild the Griffith for driving, so some of the parts on the car are not necessarily original, but installed for reliability. *Chris Hilgers*

local car guys to get their cars airborne. "The car would have broken in half," he says. "When we got the car home and started to do a careful inspection, it was much worse than I had anticipated."

He found out that Griffiths have round chassis tubes that are not much heavier than exhaust pipe tubes. On the early Series 200 models, like Hilgers', some of those tubes were bonded directly into the fiberglass body tub, which caused them to rust out rather severely. So Hilgers disassembled the entire car and had to rebuild much of the chassis.

"It was in such sad condition that when the previous owner stopped by one day while I was working on the car in my driveway, he became embarrassed and gave me a good chunk of my money back," Hilgers says. "But basically the chassis was toast, and because it sat under a leaking tarp all those years, the inside became an aquarium."

Hilgers removed the high-performance 289 engine, four-speed gearbox, and small independent rear end and stored them in his garage. Instead he installed a crate 300-horsepower, 302-cubic-inch engine, a Tremec five-speed transmission, and an 8.8-inch independent rear from a late-model Thunderbird. He also installed Minilite wheels instead of the original wire wheels because they were so worn. Now weighing in at just 1,950 pounds, the car has a very nice horse-power-to-weight ratio.

"The car is such a nice driver; very planted on the road," he says. "Every year we drive down to Monterey for the historic races at Laguna Seca. Last year we drove the Griffith for the first time. We pulled in front of the hotel, which is kind of upscale, and it was interesting to see the reactions of the car guys out front."

"These two guys walked up and said, 'Well, we were impressed that your car hadn't been painted yet, then we saw that there was no interior, but it wasn't until we saw that there was no back window that we realized that this car was a winner.' We all had a good laugh."

Hilgers hopes to have a shiny new silver paint job on his Griffith in the near future, but for now, he and his wife, Wendy, are satisfied just driving it every Sunday morning, sans paint, interior, and rear window, to the local diner for breakfast.

Car No. 2, 1953 Kurtis Roadster 500S

About ten years before he acquired the Griffith, Hilgers was hunting for an unusual car to work on and spread the word around to some of his car enthusiast buddies. One friend, a former Elva racer, said he knew of a Kurtis sports car in Camarillo, California, about twenty-five miles from his Ojai hometown. "My buddy told me he knew of this guy with a Kurtis that was all apart that will never go back together," Hilgers says. "'Go make him an offer,' he said. So I did."

Hilgers and his wife, Wendy, parked in front of the man's house, and when the man opened the garage door, Wendy said, "There's no car in there." She was right. There were mechanical and body parts scattered all over the garage and yard, and the chassis was leaning against a tree. The man said that the car had been raced and the rear end was damaged, so he disassembled the Kurtis to repair it and never finished.

When Hilgers arrived to see the Kurtis, parts were spread out all over the garage and yard, and the chassis was leaning against a tree.
Chris Hilgers

It took three pickup truck loads to bring all the parts home to Ojai. "I cleared out a spot in the garage and used my surveyor's transit to find the most level spot," he says. "I used that spot as an assembly point to reconstruct the car."

He purchased this car almost twenty years ago, so the car and the parts were much less valuable than they would be now. For instance, close inspection revealed that the original Chrysler Hemi engine had a crack, so Hilgers contacted a man in Whitehall, Montana, who sold him a replacement Hemi and delivered it all the way to California for only $1,000.

Hilgers had no idea how the gentleman he purchased the car from came to acquire the car, but knows that the man had the best intentions for the restoration. Hilgers did inherit some old photographs of the car being used on the street. But he discovered intriguing information about his Kurtis one year when he drove it to the Monterey historic races and parked it in the paddock next to a bunch of friends who owned Panteras. "This guy walked over to me and said he knew my car," Hilgers says. "He said he could remember that car because it had slightly different fenders than most other Kurtises.

Loading up the Kurtis parts into his pickup truck, Hilgers made three trips bringing the one-time race car home. *Chris Hilgers*

He said that the man who owned Gray Trucking Lines in Indianapolis bought the car and campaigned it in the Indy area for a time. Then (race driver) Jimmy (Bryan) drove the car in some Midwest races, and may have once lapped Indianapolis Motor Speedway in it."

Hilgers also believes the car was once part of the Mexican Road Race Kurtis team because it has a thirty-two-gallon gas tank. "Every other Kurtis I've seen has an eight- or nine-gallon tank," he says.

It took Hilgers about a year and a half to restore the Kurtis. He worked on it on nights and weekends in his garage. After he inventoried the parts, surprisingly nearly everything was included, although some of the parts needed updating. For instance, the car originally was equipped with a Jaguar C-Type gearbox, but it was in such terrible condition that he replaced it with a Muncie unit. The car does maintain the original Halibrand Quickchange rear end and Ford axles. "It's noisy," he says, "but you can change the gears in a matter of minutes."

Hilgers did the entire restoration himself, and even painted it in his driveway.

He was amazed at the technology used in the early sports car. The car has front and rear torsion bar suspension, and it is equipped generously with Heim joints, which give it a very compliant ride.

During restoration, Hilgers was cramped while he worked in his two-car garage. Notice his newly purchased Hemi engine on the stand to the right. *Chris Hilgers*

Since the car was built in the Glendale, California, area—near many aircraft manufacturers—the hardware is mostly of aircraft quality.

These days, Hilgers uses the Kurtis nearly every weekend to make short errands around town. It makes you wonder what builder Frank Kurtis would say if he saw the car he built as a derivation of an Indy roadster running to the mini-mart to pick up a quart of milk.

Completed at last. Hilgers and his wife, Wendy, prepare to take a cruise in their newly restored 1953 Kurtis 500S. It was rebuilt with the original-style Chrysler Hemi, but Chris decided to replace the original Jaguar C-Type transmission with a more modern Muncie gearbox. *Chris Hilgers*

The Cobra in the Bedroom

My friend Henry Wilkinson is a hound dog. The guy never stops searching out interesting cars to buy. He's owned Ferraris, Porsches, even a McLaren Can Am car, but recently he's been hunting down 289 Cobras. So one day Henry calls me and asks if I'd like to join him to load up a Cobra he had just purchased in Richmond, South Carolina. I knew this would be interesting.

Henry did what any one of us could do to find a Cobra: he ran an ad in *Hemmings Motor News* that simply read: "Wanted, 289 Cobra, any condition."

We've all seen these ads, but they don't really work, do they?

One day in May 2004, Henry received a call from Major Gerald Malloy, a U.S. Army soldier and a Cobra fanatic. Malloy, who lives in Richmond Hill, South Carolina, was jogging around his neighborhood in November 2002, and noticed what appeared to be a Cobra under a tarp, behind a Model A Ford. He said that with all the junk piled on top of the car, it was hard to tell for sure what the car was from the road. But a small portion of the car cover had lifted and exposed a rectangular taillight and the end of the bumper.

"I jogged by again and again, and decided to just knock on the door," Malloy says. "I introduced myself and asked if it was a Cobra. The gentleman, Ken Weir, said yes. I asked if I could look at it, and again he said yes."

Weir was retired from the air force, so he and Malloy had some things to talk about. Weir told him that he had purchased the Cobra in England in 1965, then moved it with him to his new station in Spain, then to Florida and Maine, where it had last been driven in 1984. He told Malloy that he hoped one day to restore it.

"From that moment, I dropped by to talk to Ken every five months or so," he says. "Then, in February 2004, I drove by and noticed that the carport was cleared out and the Cobra was gone. I almost had a heart attack." Malloy was relieved to find out that Weir had simply moved the Cobra into the house—into a spare bedroom into which he built a moveable wall. Now the car was much more viewable, without all the junk and the car cover piled on top.

Weir showed Malloy all the paperwork and serial numbers on the car. It was in fact a rare COX model. The Shelby American Registry shows that a total of fifty-nine COX—which stands for CObra eXport—cars were manufactured. These were left-hand drive Cobras, manufactured by A.C., for sale in Europe. COX6057 was originally painted Guardsman Blue and had black interior and it was consigned to a Mr. H. R. Owen, one of London's premier Rolls-Royce dealers. Weir purchased the car on July 5, 1965, and eventually brought the car to the United States. That's as much as the register tells.

Being a Cobra fan, Malloy wanted to own the barn . . . umm, bedroom, find, but with his retirement from the army pending and the recent purchase of a new house in Boston—plus his Richmond Hill home—Malloy regrettably could not consider the car. So when Henry

At least when this Cobra was put to sleep, it was put in a bedroom instead of the normal barn. COX6057, long sought after by Cobra collectors, had spent a number of years first in a Savannah, Georgia, carport, then took up residence in a spare bedroom. *Tom Cotter*

Dreams are made of scenes like this; less than seven months after this photo was taken, new owner Henry Wilkinson had totally restored this car to its original Guardsman Blue paint scheme. *Henry Wilkinson*

Wilkinson's Cobra want ad appeared in *Hemmings Motor News*, it caught Malloy's attention. When he told Wilkinson about the COX Cobra, Henry flew in his own plane the next day from Asheville, North Carolina, to inspect and purchase the car.

I was lucky enough to have been invited for the car's unveiling. As I drove up to the modest house in a pretty seaside community, the bedroom wall was just being removed. And there it was, like the opening of a tomb to unveil valuable treasures inside.

The car was no longer blue. It was now white with burgundy stripes. The doors were removed and the car obviously had been neglected for many years. But as we started to inspect the critical locations around the car for the COX6057 designations, we knew it was the real McCoy—an honest-to-goodness lost and discovered Cobra.

Henry paid a fair price for the car, including a generous finder's fee to Malloy, and then we loaded it on the truck and were headed down the road toward Henry's home several hours away. When

Wilkinson got home, he called Cobra Registrar Ned Scudder who remarked, "Eureka, you've found the lost Weir Cobra!"

In all honesty, the car did need work. Even though the trend lately is to leave Cobras in their as-found condition, this car was probably beyond that. The body had pockmarks and bad Bondo repairs, the chassis had surface rust, and the engine looked like squirrels had lived in it. Henry had the car torn apart within just a few days and worked to get parts refurbished by craftsmen throughout the region.

In less than six months, the chassis, body, suspension, and engine were all restored and simply needed assembly. The car—now finished—has become a fabulous example of the unusual COX series of Cobras and won Best of Class at the 2005 Amelia Island Concours.

And what about Malloy? Is he upset about not being in a position to buy the car of his dreams? "If I had been offered the car one month earlier or four months later, it would have been mine," he says. "But my wife believes I'll find another one, so I'm hopeful."

The Abarth Biposto

BY RICK CAREY

Miles Morris, then head of Christie's International Motor Cars Department, called in the late spring of 2003.

"Rick," he said, "I wonder if you'd do a little job for us?" I'd written auction catalog descriptions for Miles, his colleague Malcolm Welford, and their predecessor at Christie's, David Gooding, so this wasn't out of the ordinary—yet a little early for Christie's next motor cars auction at Rockefeller Center in early June. "We're consigning a car that's been sitting for about thirty years in a barn up near you, and I wonder if you'd be willing to go over, air up the tires, push it outside, take some photos, and write the catalog description?"

Fortunately, the answer to my first question, "Do I get paid?," was affirmative. So I said, "Sure. Where is it, and what's the car?," figuring it was something interesting but mundane, like a tired old XK120, early Corvette, or Bentley Mark VI. "Well," Miles responded, "it's in an estate and we don't have all the papers signed yet so I can't really tell you, but you'll like it . . . a lot."

Ten days later he called back. "The papers are signed and you can go see the car. Here's the name of the neighbor who's looking after the late owner's house. He has keys, will give you directions, and can let you in. The car is pretty interesting."

Tease.

"It's a 1952 Abarth 1500 with one-off Bertone coachwork designed by Franco Scaglione that was displayed at the Turin Motor Show."

Let's see, that's 1) a very early Abarth; 2) with one-off bodywork; 3) an auto show display car; and 4) designed by Franco Scaglione. Scaglione was a brilliant but low-profile designer, creator of the three Alfa Romeo BATs, extravagant aerodynamic experiments with pointed noses and curved fins that shocked the auto styling world in the mid-1950s. Franco Scaglione is one of my heroes.

An auction company rep called auto writer Rick Carey to craft an auction catalog description of a car near his home. The rep was oblique on the particulars, but told him, "You'll like it . . . a lot." He certainly did. It was a rare one-off Abarth Biposto. *Rick Carey*

I was up out of my chair in an instant, still on the phone but also pulling Abarth, Bertone, and coachwork reference books off the shelf. There it was, in each of the books, in period black-and-white shots from the Turin Auto Show, each with the same story: The first Scaglione design for Bertone, selected as the "Most Outstanding Car" at Turin in 1952, sold off the show stand to Packard and shipped to the states, subsequent history unknown.

This was no ordinary car. This was the answer to a half-century-old mystery.

Moments after hanging up with Miles, I was talking with his contact and arranging to visit first thing the next morning to assess the Abarth's condition. The rest of the evening was spent researching and wondering.

Built by Franco Scaglione for the 1952 Turin Motor Show, this car resided in a proper three-car garage just three miles from Carey's Connecticut home for more than thirty years. *Rick Carey*

I found that Peter Vack, author of *The Illustrated Abarth Buyer's Guide*, believes the Abarth 1500 Biposto is the first Fiat-based Abarth, the cornerstone of a long and illustrious collaboration between the Austrian-born Carlo Abarth and Fiat. Based on the short-lived Fiat 1400 platform and bearing typical Abarth tuning tweaks like free-flow exhaust and a pair of Weber Tipo 36 downdraft carburetors, its short-stroke four-cylinder engine was a much better basis for Scaglione's aerodynamic interpretations than the tall, long stroke Alfa Romeo 1900s upon which the BATs were built.

It has all the elements of a BAT (the acronym stands for Berlina Aerodinamica Technica): large central headlight flanked by grilles and peaked front fenders with smaller headlights; light and graceful roof with raked windshield and side glass; central spline down the rear glass; cutaway wheel wells; and delicate, intricately sculpted rear fender fins that gently urge airflow back across the rear deck to merge with the flow over the roof.

Scaglione had no wind tunnel. His aerodynamics were intuitive, a visually pleasing expression of fluid flow around a solid object that had to include practical elements, such as wheels, radiators, occupants, and windows. They are sensual without being voluptuous, implicitly effective without artifice. The 1952 Abarth 1500 Bertone Biposto is one of the cornerstones of aerodynamic automobile design.

How could such a significant—and visually striking—car have simply disappeared for fifty years, yet survive in, I was told, sound, complete, and nearly original condition? Subsequent research, with invaluable help from the archivists at *Fortune* magazine, revealed the story.

Bill Graves, Packard's engineering vice president, and Edward Macauley, its chief designer, had gone to Turin in 1952 looking for design ideas to freshen up Packard's bulky postwar cars. They weren't successful, but were so struck by the Abarth Biposto that they bought it and brought it back to the United States in hopes that it would provide some inspiration. Their quest didn't succeed. However, in 1952 a young *Fortune* writer, Richard Austin Smith, came to Detroit to write a story about Packard's prospects under its new president, James C. Nance, recently brought in from GE's Hotpoint appliance division.

Smith saw the Abarth and was intrigued with it, even recounting its story in his article and using it as the setting for a photo of Packard executives in which Nance was quoted describing its style as "lunar asparagus." During the visit, Smith also offered some suggestions for advertising slogans while meeting with Packard's advertising VP. After they were picked up and used, Nance wrote to Smith, offering to pay him for his creativity. Smith responded that as a *Fortune* employee, he couldn't accept payment from the subject of an article, whereupon Nance proposed to give him "the Abarth foreign car . . . to compensate you even though I know that the assistance you gave us was not done with this in mind." He also reminded Smith that he'd have to pay taxes on the Abarth's value on Packard's books: $100. The original letters were in Richard Smith's files. Nance's

This Biposto two-seater was purchased by Packard's engineering and styling department to provide the company with inspiration for future models. *Rick Carey*

letter offering to give the Abarth to Smith bore the approval initials of *Fortune*'s senior editors, along with a short note, "Enjoy the car."

He apparently did, because he preserved it carefully even while driving it enough that its odometer showed 31,926 kilometers. His children remembered their father picking them up at school in the Abarth and being the center of attention when he did. Some years later, he and his wife retired to an eighteenth-century farmhouse on the eastern Connecticut shoreline. They built a new, tight three-car garage, and thirty years ago drove the Abarth Biposto into the center stall where it stayed until 2003.

We opened the garage door early on a cold and dreary New England April morning. There sat the Biposto, dusty and neglected, but miraculously complete. I think I entered a zone walking around it, translating the few photographic images into impressions of the real thing, the genuine article. Unseen by the world at large for a

Packard eventually sold the Abarth to a *Fortune* magazine writer for $100 sometime in the 1950s. In 2004 it sold for $293,500 at the Christie's auction in as-is condition. The car now resides in England. *Rick Carey*

half-century, there it was, carefully and so obviously lovingly preserved by Richard Smith, a hundred-dollar car that was so much more. Richard Smith was no megabuck collector with a barn full of treasures. He wasn't even a hoarder, buying up neglected hulks in the hope they'd someday fund a lavish retirement. He had two cars in his garage: the Abarth Biposto and a 1998 Ford Taurus.

A few days later, we came back to take photos. The weather was still crummy, with snow lingering in the bushes and the ground sodden over a layer of frost. A cedar tree had grown up outside the garage and the Abarth's brakes were stiff. Even four of us could barely push it outside and it was a tight fit between the cedar and the garage door. We didn't even think to maneuver the Biposto into a more photogenic location. All we wanted was to take some documentary shots, then push it back inside and go get a cup of hot coffee, which we did.

Pushed onto a rollback in early June for the trip to New York and Christie's auction, the Biposto got its first "wash" in a generation. A chill rain fell on Rockefeller Center for the preview and Miles Morris' presentation of the Abarth to NBC's *The Today Show* audience. At the preview on Wednesday evening, lubricated by complimentary Cosmopolitans swirling through ice sculptures, a pool developed. It was a buck a person; seventeen dollars was collected.

The dealers and collectors there for the Biposto were assiduous in their assessment: a hundred thousand dollars, give or take. They were voting with their pocketbooks, not their aspirations, hoping to buy for a buck and sell for a buck-twenty-five. Others were more enthusiastic, or perhaps more Cosmopolitan. The top estimate? It was $275,000 against Christie's high estimate of $120,000.

The dealers never got their hands out of their pocketbooks because the Biposto surged right through Christie's estimate in a heartbeat and eventually sold to a phone bidder from England for a hammer bid of $260,000, a final price of $293,500 with Christie's buyer's commission. It wasn't the top sale of the evening—a Delage D8120 Cabriolet Grand Sport at $656,500 took those honors—but it was definitely the star of the show.

Now being restored in England, the Abarth 1500 Bertone Biposto is on anyone's list of the great barn finds of the first decade of this century, and it demonstrates that there really are great, wonderful, important, and beautiful cars out there waiting to be discovered.

This one was in a garage in Groton, Connecticut, only about three miles from my home.

The Low-Mileage
TV Guide State Pen Corvette

BY JEFF SHADE

As the host and producer of an automotive TV show, *Classic Car Garage,* I get emails from enthusiasts worldwide with questions and comments on just about everything related to collector cars. One recent email caught my interest. It was from a young lady, Tami Turnbull, who told me her father had a 1954 Corvette with, believe it or not, 1,368 original miles! At first I was skeptical, but I replied anyway with some questions about the car and how her father came to own it. She wrote back with a few photos and an offer to speak personally with her dad to get the whole story. And what a story it was. . . .

Duane Turnbull has always had more than a passing interest in cars. He's owned more than 100 collector cars of all makes and models, but he has a particular interest in Corvettes. He has owned a total of fourteen of them since 1967. His 1954 Corvette story begins when he was a high school student in McKeesport, Pennsylvania, in 1959. Duane drove a '50 DeSoto that needed brake work. His friend, who was a vo-tech student, offered to fix the brakes for him. So Turnbull gave the car to his friend for the needed work. Unfortunately, the DeSoto ended up deposited next to a light pole in the school parking lot where it sat and sat without getting the promised work done. Every time Turnbull drove by the school, he would see the car sitting in the same space, next to a pole, without ever appearing to have been moved.

Fast forward to late 1999. Turnbull traveled back to his home-town to look at a 1954 Corvette that was for sale. It was being sold by the uncle of one of his best grade-school friends. He was initially looking for a '53 parts car to help with the restoration of a '53 Corvette he already owned. When he arrived in town, he was told the '54 could be found in the old McKeesport Vocational High

School parking lot he knew so well. When Turnbull arrived to see the car, he was shocked to find the Corvette sitting in the exact same spot, next to the pole, where his '50 DeSoto had languished forty years earlier. It seemed meant to be.

What he found was a ragged looking, red Corvette with bubbling paint and neglected upholstery that was wearing 1957 Illinois license tags. Upon inspecting the car, Turnbull noticed the odometer read 1,368 miles. He thought it couldn't be right. It must be 101,368 miles. All the panels seemed to be aligned and near straight, not worn, and the steering wheel was free of wear, except for some weather deterioration. The rubber on the pedals seemed to be new also. It was missing side windows, hubcaps, and some tools from the trunk. The chrome was pitted, but the stainless was straight. Turnbull eventually left without buying the car and continued driving on a business trip to Tennessee. All the way, he thought about the Corvette and the odometer reading. Could that possibly be right? Was it possible that these crazy stories about people finding such treasures are sometimes true? Upon arriving in Tennessee, Turnbull decided to take a chance and buy the car. Not convinced that the mileage was correct, the intended purpose for the '54 was as a parts car for his '53!

Turnbull had the car transported to his home in West Virginia, where the car was stored in a trailer over the winter. Upon closer inspection of the car, he decided that the '54 was in better shape than the '53 to which it was originally intended to donate parts.

In June 2000, Turnbull sent the car off for restoration to Bill Kuhn of His Place, a highly regarded Corvette restoration shop in Emmitsburg, Maryland.

Bill Kuhn has been in business for more than forty years, with a specialty in Corvettes. Upon inspecting "every nut and bolt that holds it together," he was astonished at the authenticity of the nearly fifty-year-old sports car. The wiring was original and untouched. The shocks were the original spiral-type that weren't available after about 1955. The mufflers and tailpipes had the original factory paint on the top-side. Even the grease packing in the wheel bearings was clear! All the things that are normally replaced with use, such as belts, hoses, tires, and sparkplugs, were the original factory items and in "like-new" condition.

Bill was certain now that the 1,368 miles noted on the odometer was indeed authentic. He had a very important car on his hands and let its owner know what it was: possibly the most original and lowest mileage survivor of the entire 1953 to 1955 Corvette run, which numbered under 5,000 cars.

With this exciting news, Turnbull began a quest to locate the extensive documentation he had heard existed for this rare Corvette. With determination, persistence, countless hours of legwork, and modern computer technology, Turnbull slowly but surely unfolded the car's fascinating ownership history.

He discovered that this special '54 Corvette actually started its life "Polo White" with a red interior. In early 1955, *TV Guide* sponsored "The Long Gray Line" contest on a local Chicago TV station. Details of the contest aren't known. However, *TV Guide* wanted to give away a red Corvette, but the one given to them by Chevrolet was white. So they had a local dealer, Merit Chevrolet, paint their giveaway car red. On the evening of March 21, 1955, a Western Union Telegram from *TV Guide* arrived at the Chicago home of Robert E. Schroeder informing him that he was the lucky winner of the car. Mr. Schroeder appeared on *The Tom Duggan Show* to receive the keys. The story goes that the winner drove the car for about 300 miles total and decided he didn't like it, so he gave it to his sister. She then put about 1,000 miles on it before deciding that she too didn't like the way the car drove.

Although stylish for 1954, these early Corvettes had poor ride and handling characteristics. Around 1957, the Corvette was put away in a barn/shed building behind the Schroeder house where it sat for the next thirty-three years. At some point during the car's hibernation, the front of the building's roof collapsed exposing the car's front end to the elements.

Many people had heard about the Corvette over the years, but Mr. Schroeder would never let anyone in the storage barn to see it.

His reasons are forever unknown, but he was very meticulous about keeping records. As a result, he retained every tag, document, and bit of documentation that ever existed for the car. He had the original invoice with "N/C" (no charge) for the cost, as it was a promotional giveaway. Also in his possession were trivial items, such as the radio instructions, the cigarette lighter tag, engine break-in instructions, and the original telegram informing him of his win.

According to Social Security records, Schroeder died in 1992, so Turnbull was never able to speak with him or his family about the car. Around 1990, the car got into the hands of Pro Team Corvette, a dealer in Napoleon, Ohio. A Pro Team spotter at the 2003 Atlantic City Auction, where the car was displayed, told Turnbull he was one of the original people to travel to Chicago to remove the Corvette.

The car was then sold to a Pennsylvania man and his wife in December of 1990. How the original owner was persuaded to sell will never be known. The second owner, who shall remain anonymous, never got to do much with the Corvette. It seems his plans were cut short by a stint in federal prison on racketeering charges. As a result, the car was seized by the feds sometime thereafter and came into the possession of a company called the Vectura Group.

On September 16, 1999, Duane Turnbull finally purchased the car from his childhood friend's uncle, who represented the Vectura Group. He is now the third owner. Whew! Did you follow all that?

Obtaining the true story and tracking down the original documents was quite a detective job in itself. It took several years to finally get all of it. For nearly three years, Turnbull searched for the name of the second owner. He finally had the idea to track down the man who notarized the original paperwork. With the help of some web detective software, Turnbull was able to locate the phone number of the notary in Pennsylvania. As it turned out, he was an insurance agent for the second owners and said he would try to find a phone number.

Upon successfully getting the number, Duane called. But each time he called, someone would hang up and refuse to speak with him. Not giving up so easily after three years, he called again and again. He discovered that sometimes the answering machine he got would kick over to a fax tone. So he faxed a letter offering to pay $1,000 for the documentation if they had it. He got no immediate reply. On February 8, 2003, Turnbull received a call from the twenty-five-year-old son of the second owner. He said that his mother received his fax letter and had indeed retained the original documents. He agreed to speak with his dad, who was by then released, but thought they could make a deal.

On February 12, 2003, Duane Turnbull received a call from the man who was the second owner. They had a brief chat that resulted in the sale of the much sought-after documentation.

The Corvette's full story and documentation all came together one week before the Taj Mahal auction in Atlantic City on February 20, 2003. By then, Turnbull had had his fun with the car and was ready to sell it. While a tremendous snowstorm kept most of the bidders away, a few were there and the '54 Corvette was bid to a "no-sale" of $102,000!

Since then, the car has received a National Corvette Restorers Society restoration using one of its judging manuals. All of the original parts and markings have been preserved. Since the original lacquer paint was no longer available, it was painted its original white using a base coat and clear coat. Several NCRS judges provided divided opinions on this issue.

Because of the authenticity of the mileage, and the fact that this is the lowest mileage 1953 to 1955 Corvette known, it represents one of the rarest Corvettes in existence. It is even more rare because it retains so many original parts that were often replaced in the first couple of years of use, including sparkplugs, plug wires, tires, tailpipes, and shocks.

So keep your eyes peeled for those barns, and ask around small towns about old cars. When you find your hidden treasure, give me a call. I need more "car-in-the-barn" stories to get my car buddies through the next winter.

—Jeff Shade is the producer and host of *Classic Car Garage*.

A Rotting Relic

BY GARY STELLERN

I've been a member of the National Woodie Club since 1978. About that time, I purchased a 1947 Ford woody and began the long reconstruction process. This was a period when you could buy parts cars for a few hundred dollars, and even a respectable project car for well under $1,000. I needed parts for my new acquisition but didn't have much money. Used parts were far cheaper than new ones.

So I often read the *Woodie Times* magazine, looking for a bargain. One day an ad appeared for one and one-half parts cars in Billings, Montana. I called the person and we discussed what was available and a ballpark price. I finally asked him to hold them for me and sent a down payment, intending to drive up during the summer and tow it all back.

A few weeks prior to my departure, I noticed a magazine ad for old cars for sale just across the border in Montana, at a ranch called the Big Timber and Cattle Company (if my memory serves me correctly). I called this fellow (let's call him Bill) and we spoke of cars, etc., and when I told him of my forthcoming trip, he invited me to drop by, stay a night or so, and view the old cars he had. I did just that. The BTCC was now a dude ranch, having been settled in the late 1800s as a cattle and timber harvesting business by the present owner's great grandfather.

The owner was extremely affable and had many stories to tell of that region, some that he had lived through and others endured by previous family members. One magnificent story he told was as follows:

For many years, he had heard of an old Duesenburg touring sedan that was owned by a rancher with a large spread across the state line in Wyoming. The car had been parked on the top of a hill years ago and was never driven. This tale kept cropping up over the years as Bill grew up, and later as he began collecting cars. He finally decided to check out the story's authenticity.

He traveled south, knowing the location of the ranch, and upon arriving wasn't quite sure how to approach the owner about the "phantom" car. Bill was welcomed into the family home, but the ranch owner was a little stand-offish for the first few minutes. However, when the Montana man began talking of his family ranch and their history over the past century, the Wyoming rancher visibly relaxed. Finally Bill posed the crucial question: Is it true there is a Duesenberg parked out on a hilltop simply rusting and rotting away? The ranch owner replied that it was true and asked if the visitor would like to see the machine. The two drove out a few miles to a rounded hill and there it was: a Duesenberg, all twenty-plus feet of it, with rusting metal and rotting upholstery, slowly disintegrating.

After overcoming his astonishment, Bill asked the rancher why the car was parked here. The rancher replied that the car had belonged to his father and just before he died, his father drove it out to this knoll, parked it, and told his family he didn't want it ever removed.

I didn't go to Wyoming looking for a Duesenberg, but instead for woodies and parts. And I did bring the one-and-a-half Ford woodies home to complete my restoration. But the story of that mighty Duesenberg dissolving on a Wyoming hilltop will always rank as the most incredible "barn-find" tale of my life.

A Hollywood Phantom

Roger Morrison, a Salina, Kansas, businessman, has happened upon some pretty significant cars during his long career as a collector. But the star in his collection, a 1929 Rolls-Royce Springfield Phantom I S317KP, was originally owned by another star, Hollywood actress Marlene Dietrich.

The green Rolls was given to Dietrich as a gift from Paramount Studios after her arrival in Beverly Hills, as was documented in an April 14, 1930, letter to her daughter, Papi. Dietrich and her green Rolls became quite popular in the Hollywood area, and she was photographed frequently with it both by paparazzi and for publicity materials.

Dietrich's Rolls' chassis, manufactured in Springfield, Massachusetts, was delivered in June 1929 to custom body fabricator Hibbard & Darrin in Hollywood, where the car was transformed into what became their most attractive and famous conversion. The Darrin part of the company's name stands for Howard "Dutch"

A Hollywood star! Actress Marlene Dietrich (left) and her chauffer attracted lots of attention as they toured Beverly Hills in her 1930 Rolls Royce Springfield Phantom I. The car was given to her by Paramount Studios. *Roger Morrison*

The Rolls changed ownership a couple of times, and in 1976, a restoration began in this Lakewood, Colorado, garage. The body was stripped and some plating and painting was done, but the work ended there. *Roger Morrison*

Darrin, who was well known as a custom body builder among Hollywood's elite. Darrin had designed car bodies for King Alfonso of Spain and King Leopold of Belgium and consulted with all the top European manufacturers of the day, including Daimler-Benz, Citroen, Minerva, and others. His stylish bodies were also fitted to several Duesenburgs.

Dietrich's Rolls featured doors fabricated from cast aluminum, rather than the traditional aluminum skin over a wooden framework. Paramount paid $24,000 for it in 1929, making it one of the most expensive automobiles of the day. Dietrich took delivery on November 26 of that year, which must have made for a nice Thanksgiving two days later.

Bob Creighton of Golden, Colorado, purchased the storied Rolls in the mid-1940s. The July 1, 1960, edition of *The Denver Post* had a brief story about how Creighton's sixteen-year-old niece, Patricia Jean Creighton, took her driving exam in the huge car. She had learned to drive it at her Uncle Bob's ranch, so she was familiar with the old car's handling and controls. She learned them well enough to score ninety-eight points on the exam. Creighton called the car "invaluable" to him because it reminded him of the opulent past. At the time of his niece's driver's exam, the Phantom had 64,000 miles on the odometer.

Because of the Rolls' celebrity ownership and unmolested condition, Roger Morrison believes this is one of the most significant barn finds ever. Note that the cast aluminum doors were still stripped when Morrison purchased the car. *Roger Morrison*

Creighton kept the car in his garage for many years, and when he passed away in 1974, his daughter, Darlene Ground, inherited the car. Ground's husband began restoring it by stripping the paint, having much of the chrome replated, and painting the chassis with Imron paint. That was as far as he got on the restoration. The famed Rolls-Royce then sat disassembled in a Lakewood, Colorado, garage for twenty years.

"People in the hobby know that I'm a person who likes undiscovered cars with interesting histories," Morrison says. When California collector car dealer Charles Crail phoned Morrison in 1995 and asked if he might be interested in the car, Morrison didn't hesitate. "I bought it without ever seeing it."

Part of this find's special appeal for Morrison is the fact that this car, with its world-class design and celebrity ownership, remained undiscovered for more than fifty years. "Most cars of this sort pass from one collector to another and appear in many different color schemes over the course of their existence," he says. But Dietrich's extraordinary Rolls-Royce took a different path, from Beverly Hills' glitz and glamor, to a Colorado ranch, and then to a garage in a Denver suburb. There, this "barn find" sat for two decades before emerging for a comeback role and a return to its former splendor.

CHAPTER FOUR

Childhood Dreams

Going Backwards

BY JOHN WALCEK

I was born right when the American heyday of cars began—1950. My dad had an interest in cars, and he imparted that to his kids so much that in my teens, my older brother got a '32 Ford parts car with frame and flathead engine. Then my dad purchased a '58 Ford Skyliner with a retractable hardtop. Later we all learned to work on and drive Dad's newly purchased '59 Ford station wagon.

Then Dad got a '63 Lincoln Continental convertible. The Lincoln had a noisy engine lifter and we helped remove the engine and take everything apart. I remember all the hoses and parts and thought, *How is this ever going to get back together?* Sure enough, the

Lincoln became a permanent fixture in our garage with the parts all taped together in boxes in various places.

My interest in cars carried into my adulthood. After college when I was on my own, I purchased my first car in 1974—a '63 Galaxie Fastback. Later I purchased other cars from the 1960s, mainly convertibles. I was initially known as "Galaxie John" at the local auto parts store and later as "Lincoln John" or "Junkyard John." When I purchased the family home in 1978, the deal included the disassembled '63 Lincoln convertible in the garage. With the help of a mechanically inclined roommate, I managed to get the car back together and running, and I became preoccupied with Lincolns. Different cars came and went over the years, and I never lost money on them.

In 1995, I got a call from Ken Tibbot, a member of the Early Ford V-8 Club, to take pictures for a car calendar for its national meet in 1999. It was a great project, and I became aware of other collectors. Seeing their hobby car collections and organization inspired me. It turned out that Ken had an unrestored 1940 Lincoln Continental Cabriolet. I really took a liking to the styling, especially the distinctive

John Walcek celebrates the purchase of his 1941 Lincoln Continental Cabriolet in 2002, after the car had lived in a musty corner of this dusty junkyard shed for many years. A longtime Lincoln enthusiast, Walcek pursued the car when he heard that the junkyard's owner had died. *John Walcek*

waterfall grill. I looked at a couple of '41 Lincoln coupes over the years, but $10,000 seemed too much for me and the condition of the older cars was worse than my 1960s cars. I settled for the Franklin Mint die-cast model of the 1941 Lincoln Continental. It took up less space than the real thing!

In 1996, my daughter and I were planning a camping trip to Lassen National Park in northern California. My brother sent me an article about a Lincoln junkyard collector, Richard Goodman, who lived up there. A call to Richard yielded a very friendly and welcoming response, and a visit to his junkyard became an eagerly anticipated part of my itinerary. My daughter and I drove up in my newly purchased 1962 Lincoln Continental hardtop, even though it had a troublesome engine knock: a connecting rod or wrist pin. When we arrived, I was a bit overwhelmed by the nearly 400 cars he had. My engine problem became worse, and with Richard's expert diagnosis, recommendation, and skill, we decided that he would try to perform some band-aid repairs without removing the engine, while my daughter and I rented a car and went camping for a week at Lessen. When we returned, we learned that Richard's attempt to fix the car was unsuccessful. We ended up leaving the car there for him to rebuild the engine, and we took the bus home. I picked up the car four months later and have been driving it ever since.

Five years later, I found out that Richard Goodman died through one of my friends, Chris Foults, who works extensively on 1960s Lincolns. He has helped keep me on the road many times, as well as repairing the convertible tops and windows on my cars. He had heard Richard's son was selling his dad's Lincoln parts and cars. I didn't hesitate—I placed a call to Terrance Goodman. Like his father, he was very friendly. Upon talking with him, I learned he had many Lincolns from the 1940s as well as the 1950s and 1960s. Now my real interest centered on the older 1940s Lincolns—specifically, his two 1941 Lincoln Continental Cabriolets. One was completely stripped and in pieces; the other was complete, but with a V-8 in it.

With Chris' encouragement, we went for a 600-plus mile visit to check things out. I was eager with anticipation just thinking about the possibility of getting a pre-war Lincoln Continental Cabriolet. His price seemed reasonable: $16,000 for both of them.

I recognized the area as we approached. Terrance arrived shortly afterward. I gave him a complete set of photos I had taken when I was there in 1996. He was touched, as there were pictures of his dad and his dog, Teatheart, who has also passed on. We toured around the hundreds of cars outside, brushing away spider webs and thorny bushes. Terrance then led us into three other barns, where better samples of Lincolns from the 1950s and 1960s were stored. Upon entering the second workshop, my breath was taken away and my heart skipped a beat when I spied a '41 Lincoln Continental Cabriolet convertible in a musty corner. It was surrounded by two '46 Continental coupes coated with years of accumulated dust and a healthy buildup of bird droppings on the fenders and hoods. As a photographer, the scene alone was worth a million dollars!

After taking pictures, I approached the car respectfully, like viewing a pharaoh's tomb in an ancient pyramid, and looked it over. It was rough but appeared complete. I couldn't afford both of them, and Terrance and I agreed on a deal for the car. I gave a deposit and we wrote up a contract. He would transport the car later, using a good home-built car trailer that his dad had made. Chris and I departed for home at 2:30, some two-and-a-half hours later than planned and seven-and-a-half-hours from home. The entire way home I was dazed with disbelief. We should have had the money and transportation right there. What if he changes his mind? I won't believe it until it's home in my garage.

I didn't sleep much for the next week, preparing financing and space in my garage. Telephoning back and forth to Terrance, we arranged the specifics of getting the car to me. On Sunday, July 14, 2002, I flew from L.A. to Sacramento. Terrance picked me up and I met his wife, three kids, and his mother, Peggy, whom I'd met in 1996. She commented that she was happy to see "Connie" (their name for this particular Lincoln Continental Cabriolet) go to a new home to someone who cared, like me. We got an early start on Monday, July 15, and drove one hour out to his collection site. We loaded up the car, a V-12 engine, and miscellaneous parts.

During the process, the forklift got stuck taking the V-12 engine out of the back seat of the 1946 Lincoln. Threading a pickup truck through hundreds of dead cars in the yard was an accomplishment in itself, along with pulling the rear end of the forklift to free it from its trench. We were on the road by 9 a.m.

During the trip south, every time we stopped for gas, like a magnet, a curious crowd would gather around our treasure-in-tow, inquiring, "What kind of car is that?" and "Where did you get that?" The worst part of the trip came in the late afternoon, the hottest part of the day as we approached the grapevine, leaving the central valley. Thank God this week wasn't as hot as the 105-degree high of the previous week. As we gained altitude, the pickup's temperature crept up, but the outside air temperature decreased. We slowed down and the temperature stabilized. We made it over the hills into L.A. and home to Orange County by 8 p.m. We were definitely on a successful roll.

Now a cleaned-up 1941 Lincoln Continental Cabriolet resides in my garage. I don't know how or when I'll be able to start upgrading my purchase, as I am preoccupied with paying for it. I've got to change my life, sell some of my '60s project cars, as they pale in comparison to this rare, unique, diamond-in-the-rough, this "Pearl of Great Price": Car No. 256 of 400 Lincoln Continental Cabriolets built in 1941. How many are left or accounted for? I'm not familiar with pre-war cars, or flathead V-12 engines with six-volt positive ground systems, built before I was born, but I'm going to learn.

I need all the help I can get. I don't think I can lose. I'm on a high . . . at the end of the rainbow . . . and definitely going backwards in my life! And thanks goes to Terrance Goodman . . . and my father, for inspiring dreams and helping them come true.

A Grade School Tudor

BY TOM MILLER

I attended grade school at St. Stephens Lutheran School on the corner of Lawndale and Chamberlain in Detroit and graduated in 1965. During my grade school years, I became pretty good friends with one of my classmates who lived a block away from the school. We used to talk about what we wanted to do when we grew up. He wanted to play professional sports—one of his older brothers was in the Detroit Tiger farm system—and I wanted to work on cars.

One day in 1963, my classmate told me that their uncle gave his brother an old car. He wasn't sure what it was and didn't really care about it. Since I was only thirteen years old, I was too young to pursue it.

When I was fifteen, I purchased my first car, a 1931 Model A slant windshield town sedan for $260. The car was barely drivable. My father insisted that the car be reliable and safe before I ever drove it. One of the fondest memories I have of my dad is the time we spent together on that car. He never turned a wrench. He wanted me to learn how to do it on my own, but he was always there if I had a question.

When I finally got my driver's license, the Model A was ready to go. One of my first trips was to my good old buddy's house on Chamberlin. My buddy came outside to see my car and calmly reminded me that, "We have something like that," and he took me to the garage. It was the car he told me his brother had inherited from his uncle years earlier: a 1933 Ford DeLuxe Tudor Sedan. I looked the car over and walked away. I was in love with my Model A, and had no interest in the '33 DeLuxe. After high school, my buddy and I lost touch with each other. To this day, we have never seen each other again.

Years later, I began to think about the '33 Ford. Many times I thought that I should knock on the door and see if the car was still in there, but I thought the odds were against me. I knew that my buddy's parents had passed on, and the house was probably sold. I never did knock.

In June 2003, I happened to be driving past the school and noticed that the church was holding a garage sale to help raise funds for some special purpose. I stopped my car and used the garage sale as an excuse to go into the school and reminisce. The people inside were very friendly and I talked to them for quite a while. We talked about the good old days and pretty soon my buddy's brother, who had been in the Tiger farm system, joined us.

We talked for a while, and I told him I remembered stopping over at his house and looking at the old car in the garage. He looked at me and said that the car was still there! One of his brothers had bought the house from his parents and was still living there. He went on to inform me that his uncle bought the car brand-new in 1933 and it was his only car for thirty years. In 1963, the uncle, who

Tom Miller first saw this 1933 Ford DeLuxe Tudor Sedan in 1963, when he was a kid. It was owned by his friend's older brother. At the time, Miller had no interest in the car, but as time went on, he wondered what had become of it. *Tom Miller*

was then eighty-four years old, decided it was no longer safe for him to drive. So he gave the car to his nephew and the car was moved to Chamberlin, where it sat for forty years. That is, until I bought it. I consider myself the second owner, since the uncle and I are the only two people who have ever driven the car.

As you can imagine, the actual purchase of the car was not easy. The car was the last connection to the beloved uncle, and the owner thought the car had enough value for him to retire comfortably when the car was sold. As I recall, negotiations took all of five months. It was four months of calling, leaving messages, and waiting for return calls before I could even look at the car. The owner explained that he was trying to find an appraiser to come out and place a value on it. He even called the Henry Ford Museum in an attempt to get one of their people out to appraise the car. I do not know why, but no appraiser ever came out.

I finally convinced the owner to let me look at the car by saying that, depending on the condition of the car, I might not even want it. Why should we waste our time, I told him, if I would not be interested in purchasing the car in the first place? When I finally did get the opportunity to go, I took along a copy of *Hemmings* and an old car price guide. I looked the car over and decided it was desirable, and that I would like to have it. I knew that he would not trust the offer I gave him as a fair price, so instead of making him an offer, I showed him a reasonable price range for a vehicle in the condition the car was in based on my reference material. He indicated that he had a price in mind that just happened to match the highest number in the range I just showed him. I anticipated his reaction and countered with convincing evidence to justify a lower price. As I was leaving, he indicated his bottom line to me and I told him that I would think about it.

I was reasonably convinced that his bottom line price was fair. A couple of days later, I called him and told him that I had to look at the car again. He said he would meet me the next Saturday morning. I went to the bank, took out his bottom line in cash, and arranged for a friend to follow me in a trailer. As my friend and I looked over the car, he whispered in my ear, "If you do not want this car, I'll take it." I handed the owner my bundle of cash, and he presented me with the title and the original keys still in his uncle's key case.

The Ford had 51,243 miles showing on the odometer. The only things missing were the radiator cap and the air cleaner. (Both of which I am still looking for.) The engine turned freely. The original tire pressure gauge was in the glove compartment, and the tool bag—complete with most tools—was on the floor. I believe that everything on the car was original except the tires. The sheet metal was extremely straight with the exception of the fenders that had minor "garage dings." The paint was extremely faded and even absent in some areas; I call it "patina." Someone had covered the car with a sheet of plastic, which I believe trapped moisture next to the car and caused the paint and the chrome to degrade.

As soon as I got the car home, I filled up the tires. They held air and still do. I removed, cleaned, and reinstalled the oil pan and fuel tank. I was able to remove all the fasteners except one without using heat. The oil pan was full of scale and sludge, and the fuel tank still had half a gallon of stale gasoline in it. To this day, my garage smells like that stale gasoline! I changed all the fluids, lubricated everything, repaired the fuel gauge, and replaced the kingpins and bushings. I replaced the Detroit Lubricator carburetor with a Stromberg, having changed the intake manifold with one from a '36 Ford, and added a new fuel pump. I then cleaned the points, pulled the sparkplugs, and injected oil into each cylinder. I took a battery from an old Farmall tractor I have and spun the engine over until I had oil pressure, then installed new plugs. I threw some gas into the carburetor and turned the ignition on. The engine cranked about half a turn and she was running. She sounded pretty good, too.

I called the person I had just bought the car from and held the phone to the engine. He was excited to hear the car run again, and he remembered his uncle driving the car all those many years ago when he was a kid. I was shocked to find the horns, ammeter, and

A chance meeting at a school function forty years later put Miller back in touch with his friend's older brother. After he purchased the Ford, he realized that it was one of the most original and complete '33 Fords around. *Tom Miller*

lights all functioning. I found an old Vernor's Ginger Ale bottle between the front seats, and a pair of knit gloves under the driver's seat that disintegrated when I picked them up.

It didn't take long before the engine started to overheat. I had quite a problem with rust in the block breaking loose and clogging the radiator. I have had the radiator out three times so far for cleaning. I finally made an attachment for my garden hose that, when inserted in the lower water outlet or water pump mounting surface, can reach all the way to the back of the block or head. I was able to flush a great quantity of rust out in this manner. Except for a broken tooth on second gear, I think everything will be okay as soon as I get the brakes straightened out. I plan on leaving the car pretty much like it is, even though everything is faded and worn. I believe I have an obligation to leave the car as original as possible. Besides, with two kids in college, I'm broke! It would be tough for me to come up with the money for a top-notch restoration. The only other things I might eventually replace is the tires because they are in pretty bad shape.

Now, if I could only find a '34 Cabriolet. . . .

The Discovery of Splinter

BY GARY WOOLERY

My flashlight beamed across the room and caught a reflection. The shiny object came into focus—it was an emblem of an Indian on a hubcap. Objects littered the ground, which concealed the hubcap's owner. My curiosity mounted with each box that I moved, until I revealed that the hubcap was not alone.

What appeared to be wooden crates stacked up in this old warehouse was actually a car. I had discovered a 1938 Pontiac woody station wagon. Although it was badly damaged from decades of abandonment, a core of its original splendor still existed. Looking at the car brought a wave of nostalgia as I remembered similar Indian emblems racing by me on the streets near my childhood home in suburban L.A. I thought about my popular high school friend who drove a woody. I thought about the Beach Boys and their surfing songs. This car was a treasure, even on four flat tires, with dents, a deteriorated ragtop roof, and exposed interior and exterior wood that was severely eaten by termites.

Gary Woolery found this rare eight-cylinder 1938 Pontiac woody in a Long Beach, California, warehouse. After it gave the original owner fifteen years of service in his surveying business, the car broke down and was put in storage in 1953. Woolery bought it in 1990. *Gary and Alisun Woolery*

The vintage sign displays the original owner's business on the tailgate. But look at the wood: the car was certainly a challenge to restore with all the dry-rotted and broken wood. *Gary and Alisun Woolery*

"You found my dad's old car," said a voice from behind me. I turned to see my client and executor of his father's estate. His father had been a surveyor in the city of Long Beach, a major port city in L.A. His warehouse was his main base of work, and it was just three blocks from my own business. My client told me the story of his father's car, and I came to realize how special it was. His father placed a special order to the local Pontiac dealer in 1938 for a straight eight-engined station wagon with a side-mounted spare tire. The eight-cylinder engine was beneficial for his surveying business in the old hills of Long Beach because it provided additional power. It was a true working man's car as it jostled around the rich old oil fields of the port city. In 1953, the car broke down in these hills after fifteen years of service. His father decided it would be best to buy a new car, as it would have cost at least $200 to fix up the Pontiac. But even though he purchased a new car, he could not part with his beloved woody. He kept the car until his death in 1990.

The executor, his son, now owned the car, but because of its state of disrepair, he felt it would be best to sell. He had planned to put an advertisement in the local *Pennysaver* newspaper, but I wouldn't leave the warehouse without first owning the car. I made him an offer by bartering the price of the car deducted from work that needed to be done on his father's business property. The son saved himself the trouble of finding another buyer, and I now owned a woody.

After much sanding, varnishing, and painting, the one-time warehouse woody, known to its owner as *Splinter*, looks like this today. The National Woodie Club states that four eight-cylinder 1938 woodies exist today. *Gary and Alisun Woolery*

Moving a car that had not seen the light of day since 1953 was quite an ordeal. Using a portable air compressor, I was surprised when miraculously the tires inflated enough to tow the car to my office three blocks away. The quarter-mile trip didn't seem impossible, except that in one turn, one of the doors fell off the car and into the street. The car's poor condition finally became reality as I ran into the street to retrieve the door. I began to wonder if the purchase was such a good idea.

Within months, my find had proved its worth, for it was during the restoration process that I learned more about the woody. I joined the Pontiac Oakland Club and the National Woodie Club in order to research the car, find parts, and become acquainted with fellow classic car owners. Today, a 1938 Pontiac woody is extremely rare. Most of the ones still around have six-cylinder engines, except mine! After eight years of restoration, my car is not only drivable, but it's show worthy. *Splinter*, as we affectionately refer to our car, made its first public appearance at my daughter's high school as the senior rally car through the National Charity League. Driving the car for the first time is a classic car owner's most prideful moment. *Splinter* has now been the joy of many car shows, Sunday drives to church, and special occasions. It turned out to be a lucky find.

A Twelve-Year-Old's Dream

It was 1950, and a twelve-year-old boy we'll call Bob was doing what twelve-year-olds did before the age of video games and the Internet: he was being adventurous. He was exploring the rural areas around his home on the outskirts of Columbus, Ohio, and because he was a car-crazy kid, he was searching for old cars.

Walking down the road, he came across an old barn that was just too tempting to pass by; he had to look inside. He snuck across the field, being careful not to let anyone in the nearby farmhouse see him, and he crept up to the building. He peered into the dark barn, and it took a few moments for his eyes to focus, but what he saw was to become the love of his life—a 1932 Ford roadster pickup. He noted that a name was written on the door: Borden's Golden Crest Grade A Milk. Perhaps the truck had been used for milk deliveries, or perhaps for hauling materials around the Borden farm.

Find the hidden roadster pickup! "Bob" first discovered the extremely rare 1932 Ford roadster pickup in 1950 when he was twelve years old. He finally was able to buy it fifty-three years later at the age of sixty-five! *Paul Dobbins*

Ford didn't build many Model B open-cab roadster pickups in 1932, probably for good reason. Most folks wanted a work truck to haul goods or farm supplies, or they wanted a roadster to take on Sunday drives in the summer with the top down. Very few people wanted a convertible truck. Worldwide production of open-cab trucks in 1932 was only about 600, making the '32 Ford one of the rarest and most sought-after vintage Fords on the planet. Records show that none of the pickups were manufactured with the famous flathead V-8 engine that had been introduced that year. Instead, all were produced with a four-cylinder Model B engine, a variation of the venerable Model A that had gone out of production the previous year. The trucks could be retrofitted with the V-8 at the dealership if the customer wished to pay an additional fee, which accounts for the few V-8 roadster pickups in existence.

Bob did what any excited kid would do at that moment. He knocked on the door of the farmhouse and asked if the old Ford in the barn was for sale. "Nope," said the farmer. "I'm going to fix it up one day." So Bob said thank you and went about his twelve-year-old adventures on that day in 1950.

But he never forgot about that pickup.

Year after year, decade after decade, Bob thought about that '32 Ford, and occasionally inquired with the farmer whether it was for sale yet. Every time the answer was no. Meanwhile, the truck sat obediently in the barn, out of the elements, and out of view from car collectors. It appears that only Bob knew of the pickup's presence.

In 1993, fifty-three years after Bob first discovered the roadster pickup, the old farmer passed away. By now, Bob was a sixty-five-year-old man, but his love for old cars was still as strong as that twelve-year-old kid's. He had heard about the farmer's death, and he discovered that the farmer's son had inherited the '32 Ford. He was finally able to negotiate the purchase after more than half a century of trying. Over the years, Bob had become a car collector, and annually made the pilgrimage to Hershey, Pennsylvania, for the large

Now owned by renowned '32 restorer, Russell Smith, the roadster pickup will soon undergo an authentic restoration, possibly even with the Borden's Golden Crest Milk livery logo repainted on the doors.
Paul Dobbins

parts swap meet there. During one of those trips several years after purchasing the Ford, he was selling parts at one of the booths—1932 Ford parts, in fact—when a gentleman named Russell Smith of St. Petersburg, Florida, came over to look at Bob's parts on the table. Smith mentioned to Bob that he needed parts to finish the restoration of a 1932 Ford Phaeton, but what he really wanted was a '32 Ford roadster pickup.

Bob mentioned that he had one and showed him a few photos. Smith—who is a renowned 1932 Ford restorer, and whose nickname is Deuce Smith—had to own the car and wouldn't leave Bob's booth until he negotiated its purchase.

Smith restores only the most authentic 1932 Fords, from sedans to his latest, a Wayne-bodied school bus, and he only starts with the very best candidates. He is known for not overly restoring cars, but instead making them exactly the way they were produced by Ford Motor Company.

By the time the Hershey swap meet was over, Smith owned the roadster pickup.

It is now in Florida, where Smith is researching the car's history and collecting materials for its restoration.

"When Deuce does a restoration, it is correct," says his friend Paul Dobbins, also of St. Petersburg, who helped with this story. "If it would be prettier to chrome plate the brass windshield stanchions rather than paint them black like the originals, he'll still paint them black."

Smith has even considered restoring the car in its Borden's dairy livery.

The question is: Why, after fifty-three years of lusting after an old car, did Bob ultimately sell the car? "He wasn't a twelve-year-old anymore," Dobbins says. "He had owned lots of old cars over the years, and at sixty-five, [he] was beginning to wind down."

Or, perhaps the search and discovery of the car was more gratifying than owning it.

Chance Conversation Strikes a Cord

Herb Fischer knew a little something about Cord automobiles before he actually owned one. Back in 1941, his father drove past a gas station in central New Jersey and noticed a 1936 Cord for sale. The car ran but wouldn't move, and it was for sale for $200. Fischer's father was handy with tools, so he figured he could install a new clutch and have a good-looking car to drive around. So he bought it.

Once it was home and disassembled, he discovered that in addition to the clutch being worn, the first and reverse gears in the transmission were also shot. But with the help of the Cord Company of Auburn, Indiana, his father ordered the correct parts. Thanks to those parts, plus *lots* of labor, the stylish Cord was eventually on the road again.

During World War II, while Fischer was in the service, his father stored the Cord in his garage. However, he failed to drain the engine block and it cracked. After the war, Fischer's father sold the car for $300 to someone interested in restoring the old sedan.

Fast forward twenty-five years to 1970. Fischer was now a high school industrial arts teacher and a car collector who still owned the first car he ever restored back in 1958 with his father and his brother at the family's service station near Somerville, New Jersey—a Model A Ford. "If you were restoring a car back then, your only source of parts were J. C. Whitney, Sears-Roebuck, and junkyards," he says.

"Many of my students knew I was interested in old cars," he adds. One day a student approached him and asked if he had ever heard of a Cord automobile. "His uncle had a 1936 model stored in a shed near our town and was interested in selling it," Fischer remembers.

Fischer and his son went to look at the Cord, which was stored in an old barn, blanketed in dust, but complete. "It had been sitting for a very long time, and the moths had chewed up the wool broadcloth interior," he says. "But they wanted twenty-five hundred dollars for it, which was a lot more money than I was used to paying for the old cars I bought. I was buying Model As for five hundred dollars at the time." Yet the car was very complete, and he took a chance that the car was mechanically sound, so he paid the $2,500 and called his mechanic to help him get the car home. "The seller was very encouraging and predicted that the car would one day be worth as much as five thousand dollars."

The car was towed out of the barn and to Fischer's home. It turns out that Fischer's 1936 model was the 33rd car built—a very early example of the front-wheel-drive, coffin-nose Cord. The car was purchased new by a wealthy family in Pennsylvania, and Fischer became the third owner.

"The early Cords had a provision on the cowl to fill the oil and water, but those fillers were closed off on the later Cords," he says.

Ever since he and his father had fixed up an old Cord before World War II, Herb Fischer had an admiration for the marque. In 1970, while working as a school teacher, he had a chance conversation with a student whose uncle was interested in selling a Cord he had stored in this shed. *Herb Fischer*

"The early cars also had blue leather seats with gray piping in the driver's compartment." A total of 2,500 Cord Westchester Sedans were built between 1936 and 1937. Some 1937 models were equipped with a supercharger, which was quite troublesome. The supercharged cars are easily recognizable due to their exhaust pipes that come out the sides of the hood and were designed by famed automotive stylist Gordon Buehrig. His initial intention was for the Cord to be a "baby" Duesenberg.

While owned by the original family, this Cord was involved in a fatal accident and put into storage. Later, another man in Pennsylvania purchased the car and performed some work on it, but he lost interest. "He was more into airplanes, and traded it for a Piper Cub," Fischer says.

Fischer spent a lot of time cleaning the engine and carburetor. After filling the tank with fresh gas, he finally got it running. "Then I checked the oil and it was white," he says, thinking the Lycoming-built flathead V-8 block was cracked. It turned out that it was only a blown head gasket, which he easily replaced.

Fischer had the car repainted in Cadet Gray and had a new broadcloth interior installed. He also had the car's chrome replated. The car was finished several years later, and it still runs quite well.

Fischer credits Cord expert Glen Pray of Oklahoma and the Auburn-Cord-Duesenberg Club for helping him locate parts and obtain service information.

The Cord sits in a prominent position inside his garage, next to his other collectibles: a '47 Bentley, '51 Cadillac, '57 Rolls-Royce, '51 Mercedes Cabriolet, '36 Ford Cabriolet, '41 Packard convertible, and his original project, the Model A that he purchased in 1958.

The Silver Bullet

Henry Wilkinson first saw the car of his dreams in 1968, when he was a freshman at Wofford College. He was home visiting his parents in Asheville, North Carolina, when he was passed by a silver Ferrari on Vanderbilt Road in the Biltmore Forest neighborhood where he lived. "I was driving the thirty-five-mile-per-hour speed limit, and this silver bullet comes past me at a multiple of that speed," he says. The car was a year old at the time, and he later found out that it had been purchased new by a surgeon, Dr. Robert Moffatt, who lived in the same neighborhood.

The car was a 1967 330 GTC two-place coupe, and Wilkinson instantly fell in love with it.

In the mid-1980s, long after he had graduated from college and become a successful businessman, Wilkinson found himself thinking about the Ferrari in the same way you might about an old girlfriend after a couple of decades have passed. He said to himself, "I wonder what ever happened to that car?"

Wilkinson tracked down Moffatt, who was evasive and told him that the engine had blown up and he didn't have the car anymore. Yet, several years later, Dr. Moffatt stopped Wilkinson after church and asked him to come over to his house that afternoon. When he arrived at the doctor's house, Wilkinson was surprised to find the

While he was a college student, Henry Wilkinson remembers seeing a Ferrari 330 GTC speeding by in his neighborhood. The doctor who owned it blew the engine and put it into his garage, where it hibernated for more than twenty years. Wilkinson bought it, painted it red, and sold it at the height of the Ferrari market in the late 1980s. *Henry Wilkinson*

garage door open and inside was the silver Ferrari. It turns out that the doctor's story was half correct: it did have a blown engine, but it had been parked in a standard garage and had deteriorated badly.

"The twenty years had taken its toll on the old girl," Wilkinson says. "He asked if I was still interested in buying it, and I said, 'Sure'."

After negotiating the purchase, and trailering the car home, he began a thorough analysis of his project. "The interior had rotted, the silver paint had deteriorated, and the fuel had gone bad and crystallized in the tank and fuel lines," he says. Realizing that it was a project larger than his talents, Wilkinson shipped the car off to Skip McCabe in Chicago for a ground-up restoration.

Wilkinson restored the car for the booming late-1980s Ferrari market and admits he would take a different approach today. "The car was silver from new, but I painted it red because in 1989, the market was going crazy for red Ferraris," he says.

After enjoying the car for a couple of years, Wilkinson sold it to David North of Totowa, New Jersey. That would normally be the end of the story, but a dozen years later, North was re-introduced to Wilkinson at the Amelia Island Concours in 2004. "I asked him if he still had the Ferrari, and what condition it was in," Wilkinson says. "He did still own it, but admitted to me that it was in 'ratty' condition and needed restoration. I said 'What? I sold you a concours condition car. What did you do to it?'"

"It was one of those rare cases where the guy actually drove the car!"

North used the Ferrari to commute from his house in New Jersey to his vacation home in Vermont, rolling up 60,000 miles from the time he purchased it. "He didn't care about devaluating it, but just wanted to use it as it was designed: to be a grand tourer," Wilkinson says. "Thankfully, he didn't just stick the car in the garage and use it once a year.

Who knows, if Wilkinson is lucky enough to talk North out of the Ferrari one of these days, he just might get his wish of restoring the car again—but this time in silver.

MGs in the Barn

In 1957, Nancy Moore of Lake Grove, New York, purchased a slightly modified 1948 MG TC. The previous owner had removed the front wings (fenders) and replaced them with a unique pair of cycle fenders that turned with the front wheels.

Early in her ownership of the MG, she met another car enthusiast, Dennis Sullivan, who loved the MG and also loved Ford Model Ts, of which he owned several. In 1959, Nancy and Dennis married, and the MG became their family car. They drove the MG on their honeymoon, first to Cape Cod, and then all the way up to the Canadian border.

Back on Long Island, the MG was used for commuting and shopping trips. And the Sullivans were caught up in the sports car movement of the day, so the couple thought nothing of driving the little green MG to Lime Rock and Watkins Glen to watch the road races. They often participated in pre-race parade laps.

As a car-crazy kid on a bicycle, the author of *The Cobra in the Barn*, Tom Cotter, remembers seeing this MG TC in a garage back in the mid-1960s. Thirty years later, when he peeked in the same garage door, it was still there! *Tom Cotter*

When the Sullivan children started to arrive, the MG still remained the family's favorite mode of transport. Once they packed their two small children into homemade baby seats in the small package shelf behind the seats and went to visit relatives in Potsdam, New York.

I first remember seeing the MG, in addition to the Model Ts, in the Sullivans' driveway in the mid-1960s. I was about ten years old, and I was bike riding with my friend Charles "Buzzy" Brischler in the neighborhood streets near his house. I remember a garage and driveway filled with interesting cars, which we looked at for a few moments before continuing on our ride.

Not long after we spotted those cars, the Sullivans put the MG up for sale. "When we had three children, the MG was not very useful anymore, so we put it up for sale in 1966," Nancy says. "It was purchased by a man from (nearby) Smithtown."

Nearly ten years passed, and in May 1975, Dennis died. A few months later, Nancy saw her old MG for sale in the newspaper and in a nostalgic moment, decided to buy it back. "The guy who owned it made some changes I wasn't very happy about," she says. "He stripped leather off the seats and replaced it with vinyl, and he changed the dashboard." Nonetheless, she repurchased the MG, had the exhaust system replaced, and rarely used it.

In the early 1990s, when my wife, Pat, and I were visiting my in-laws in Lake Grove, I decided to pack my young son into the car and take a ride. When I passed the house on Hawkins Avenue, I suddenly remembered the cars I had seen there as a child. So I pulled my rental car up to the curb and peeked into the garage window. "Son-of-a-gun," I said to myself—the MG and the old Fords were still in there! So with Brian in my arms, we knocked on the door of the house, and when Nancy answered the door, I told her of my bicycle ride past her house more than thirty years earlier, and wondered if I could see the MG. We walked out to see the car I hadn't seen since I was probably ten or twelve years old. Interestingly, the car started and ran nicely, since it had just been tuned up by Sullivan's son-in-law.

Owner Nancy Sullivan of New York purchased the car in the 1950s and drove it on her honeymoon and on a number of trips to Watkins Glen for the U.S. Grand Prix. It had a few slight modifications, including cycle front fenders that steer with the front wheels. *Tom Cotter*

I had to ask, "Is the MG for sale?"

Well, yes, but we couldn't come to terms on a price, so I said goodbye, gave her my phone number in North Carolina, and left. Nearly every Thanksgiving from that point forward, I would visit her with my son, who was now growing into a young man. She looked forward to my annual visits, as we'd continue our never-ending conversations on the car's value. You see, as time went on, I actually became less interested in the car. I had an MG TD at home, along with a growing car collection. However, I continued to visit and call her from time to time.

As of October 2004, the MG and the Model Ts were still sitting obediently in the Lake Grove garage. Nancy says she'd like to sell them, but I believe that deep down inside, she'd like to keep the memories alive of the good times that she and Dennis shared.

The Wrecking Yard Coupe

Dale Manning grew up in Oklahoma as a car-crazy kid. He had trusting parents, because in 1946, when he was only twelve, they let him buy a 1940 Ford coupe. He used all the money he had made doing odd jobs for the purchase, which hadn't left enough for a new battery. No problem for this twelve-year-old: he parked on hills, so he could pop the clutch and be on his way for his next drive.

When he was a little older, Manning operated a wrecking yard and transmission repair shop on four acres in Lakeside, Texas, a small community outside Fort Worth. Manning drove the coupe when he dated his wife, Darlene, and even drove it on their honeymoon.

When he purchased a new pickup in 1972, Manning still had the '40 coupe. About that time, he decided to "hot rod" it. He pulled out the old flathead V-8 and installed a 1973 Corvette engine and three-speed transmission, which was adapted to the standard 1940 Ford

This 1940 Ford coupe sat in a Lakeside, Texas, transmission repair shop from 1972 until March 2004. The deceased owner, who purchased the coupe as a twelve-year-old in 1946, had begun to modify the car, but never finished installing the front end. *Roger Morrison*

The coupe had 1960s-style rolled-and-pleated two-tone interior already installed when Roger Morrison purchased the car. Note that many of the dash items, such as the instrument cluster, have been chromed. *Roger Morrison*

column shifter. He fitted a '73 Corvette independent rear, but never completed the installation. The front end was removed to receive disc brakes, but was never re-installed. From that time until Manning's death in 2001, the car never moved from the corner of his transmission shop. By that point, the front axle had been lost, along with a number of other parts.

Over the years, numerous old car enthusiasts inquired about the car and whether it was for sale, but Manning would never sell.

Upon his death, however, his widow, Darlene, agreed to sell it to Jim Cozart, who first saw the coupe in 1981. Cozart moved it to a building he owned, where it again sat untouched until March 30, 2004. At that time collector Roger Morrison purchased Manning's old '40 Ford coupe.

"Every piece of sheet metal on the car was installed by the factory," Morrison says. "The original grille is virtually perfect and the headlight surrounds are not cracked. The stainless trim is blemish-free, and the hood, fenders, and doors all fit exceptionally well, although the 1956 Chevy Aztec Gold paint is flaking off in areas."

The car is being refurbished, with the standard Ford front and rear ends being reinstalled. The rolled-and-pleated interior, probably installed sometime in the 1950s, is in surprisingly good condition.

Once the car is running and driving, Morrison will decide whether to repaint the car or leave it with the same paint it has had for decades.

The unfinished project had a 1973 Corvette engine and a three-speed transmission installed. A Corvette independent rear suspension was also partially installed before work ceased. *Roger Morrison*

CHAPTER FIVE

Racing Relics

Lost and Found

When thinking about discovering classic cars in barns, car lovers usually visualize Packards, Duesenbergs, and Pierce Arrows, and rarely dream of an American Motors Corporation (AMC) product. But vintage racing enthusiast Steve Francis found what could be the most significant AMC road racer ever to compete in Europe one day while he was surfing the Internet.

Francis grew up first in Detroit, then in California. His father made his living as a dealer service manager for Rambler/American Motors dealerships and his mother worked in the dealer offices, so the youngster was predisposed to the "Non-Big Three" brand of cars, as he calls them. He remembers his father driving home the new Rambler Marlin demonstrators when they were first introduced in 1965 to compete against the new Mustangs and Barracudas. "One day I have to own one of those," Francis told himself. A couple of decades

After retiring from international competition, the Spirit competed in the 1981 and 1982 Daytona twenty-four-hour races and in several Kelly American Challenge races. Finally, it was used as a pace car for IMSA races before disappearing from the public eye. *Steve Francis*

later, he did buy one that was for sale in Houston. He kept it for a while until caving in under the pressure from his Mustang-owning friends who urged him to sell. Nevertheless, the die was cast for this road racing–AMC enthusiast to once again own a significant car of the brand.

It was an eBay listing that eventually caught Francis' attention. It advertised an as-found AMC Spirit race car that was located in Denver, Colorado. The photo showed a sad-looking car sitting in a driveway. He began to bid on the car, but then thought better, realizing that a November trip from Connecticut to Colorado would be a tough one. He stopped bidding and the car was sold to another bidder from Colorado, who put it in storage.

Later, Greg Taylor of Michigan purchased the Spirit, and drove from Michigan to Colorado to pick up his new gem. Taylor basically did nothing with the car, but he did discover that it had some significant racing history: it had competed in the 24 Hours of Daytona races in both 1981 and 1982. Taylor posted the car for sale in the Great Lakes Region AMC newsletter. Francis' brother spotted the ad and called him about it. The ad listed it as an AMC race car with Daytona racing history that was a "roller" and needed full restoration. Francis knew it was the car he passed up a couple of years earlier, so he bought it sight unseen.

He picked up the car in Michigan and trailered it to a nephew's house about one hour away. "We cracked open some beers to celebrate and started to pick away at the faded, old white paint," Francis says. "My brother first noticed some bright colors under the white on the quarter panels and we started to sand and pick further."

Francis quickly went into his motorhome, where he had a copy of *Automobile Quarterly*, Volume 19, No. 1, which he had purchased on eBay just a week prior. The issue contained a story about the 1979 Team Highball Nurburgring race cars, and Francis just wanted to brush up on his AMC racing knowledge.

"We were very lucky that none of the previous owners had stripped the old paint off the car," says Francis, now a Connecticut-based racing parts distributor, "because if they had, I never would have found the old painted stripes that were hiding under the twenty-one-year-old white paint job."

Those red, orange, blue, and yellow stripes were the ultimate clue. It turns out that Francis had stumbled across the long-missing, class-winning Spirit AMX from the 1979 Nurburgring twenty-four-hour race.

Holding the book against the rear quarter panel of the Spirit, Francis confirmed that he had discovered the No. 2 car. "Upon further inspection, we found the hole in the roof for the radio antenna and the rain light brackets in the rear bumper," he says. "Bingo!"

Francis' barn find was half of a two-car team that was campaigned by Amos Johnson's North Carolina–based Team Highball, a tongue-in-cheek group of racers who achieved a surprising amount of success, yet never lost their sense of humor. The two cars were prepared for the grueling twenty-four-hour race in less than three weeks from the time they were received at Team Highball's shop. These were the first-ever American entries in the legendary race on West Germany's 14.1-mile, 176-turn course.

This particular car was sponsored by both AMC and BF Goodrich Tires, and it was built for Lyn St. James, Gary Witzenburg, and Jim Downing to drive in the 1979 Nurburgring twenty-four-hour race.

Wearing a brilliant black, blue, orange, and yellow paint scheme, the car represented America well as it finished first in class, its sister car finishing second, for a one-two Team Highball win. Even more surprising, both cars competed on BF Goodrich street radial tires—a significant sales promotion for the company's new brand of high-performance tires.

Francis' car is listed as THB-307: THB stands for Team High Ball, the number 3 designates that it was built on a Spirit body, and number 07 means that it was the seventh Spirit racer built by the team. The car was an AMX model and equipped with the optional 304-cubic-inch V-8 and a four-speed transmission.

After the car's Nurburgring appearance, the Spirit AMX sat idle until late in 1980, when it was used as a pace car at an IMSA race. While being driven on a wet track with very old racing tires, the car spun into thick mud. Francis explains that race officials decided to leave the car there until after the race. "A bad decision," he says. "Not long after a restart, another racer crashed into the front of the AMX, making a real mess out of it." Francis' investigation revealed evidence of this collision.

Back at the team's Raleigh, North Carolina, headquarters, mechanics replaced the front clip with one from an IMSA Kelly Challenge AMC Concord. After this repair, the car was upgraded from

Complete with unique camshaft rear-hatch holder, the Spirit was for sale on eBay from this Denver, Colorado, driveway. Steve Francis tried to buy it then and lost out. When the same car was for sale again in the Detroit area, he bought it. *Steve Francis*

Halfway restored. Francis will campaign the Spirit in vintage sports car races and reunions when it's completed. *Steve Francis*

FIA Group 1 specs to IMSA GTO specs. The car then began to compete in the Kelly Challenge Series as well as the 24 Hours of Daytona. In 1981, it recorded a thirty-seventh-place finish at Daytona after dropping out of the race on lap 303; in 1982, it lasted 132 laps and was credited with a fifty-second-place finish.

After the 1982 season, the car was resold many times and it never raced again. Its unique history was long forgotten.

Since acquiring the car in 2003, Francis has removed the large rear fender flares that were adapted during its IMSA GTO days and welded on new quarter panels. He also located and installed NOS (new old stock) front fenders. The car has been totally sandblasted and primer painted. He has contacted both Witzenburg and St. James about a reunion with the car, and he hopes to be invited to the Goodwood Festival of Speed in 2006. St. James, who has many fond memories of the Spirit AMX, has expressed an interest in driving her old race car up the hill at Goodwood.

It would be a great fitting conclusion for a race car that was once a neglected and abused piece of driveway trash.

Stumbling upon an SCCA Champion

Steve Silverstein is a Sunbeam collector. Unlike most Sunbeam collectors, who seek out only the very desirable Ford V-8-powered Tigers, Silverstein truly appreciates the Tiger's less-powerful sibling, the Alpine. Alpine Series IVs were powered by 1600-cc four-cylinder engines that produced eighty-seven horsepower, and they were capable sports cars in their day. So capable, in fact, that the manufacturer, Rootes Group, decided to field some factory-backed entries in amateur sports car races during the 1960s against some very formidable competition from both MG and Triumph. As it turned out, the entries were surprisingly successful.

Scanning the Sunbeam Alpine Owner's Club website in early 2000, Silverstein zeroed in on a particular ad: "Alpine Race Car For Sale—Freshly Machined Engine." The machined engine caught his attention because the oil pressure in his own street Alpine's engine was on the decline. When he arrived at the owner's home, he saw

Sunbeam Alpines are not usually associated with racing, but this particular 1964 No. 74 Alpine was one of the most successful F-Production amateur race cars of its day. Here it does battle with a Porsche E-Production Speedster. *Steve Silverstein*

Don Sessler (in helmet) drove this Sunbeam to the 1964 SCCA F-Production National Championship. Here he takes one of many victory laps with his wife and crew. *Steve Silverstein*

that the car was in worse condition than he was led to believe. He suspected that the engine block was cracked and very little of the car's history was known. But there were a number of new old stock (NOS) parts included in the deal, and most of the chrome and trim pieces were in good condition, so he struck a deal for what was to be an Alpine parts car.

When the newly acquired Alpine Series IV arrived at Silverstein's Marlboro, Massachusetts, home, his wife Ellen wasn't too impressed. They began to unload boxes of spare parts onto shelves in the basement when Ellen discovered at least 100 receipts. She caught her husband's attention when she began to read some of the notes out loud: "New Koni shocks for Daytona, '67." She also found some postcards from one of the car's former owners, Dan Carmichael. An Internet search revealed that Carmichael was an accomplished road racer who raced Sunbeams for the Sports Car Forum in Columbus, Ohio.

Silverstein's interest was piqued, and he ran to his bookshelves to discover that the Sunbeam he had just purchased may have been more than simply a club racer back in the 1960s. In the book *Tiger, Alpine, Rapier* by Richard Langworth, Silverstein came across the name Don Sessler, who won the SCCA F-Production National Championship in 1964. He called Sessler and confirmed that the car he had just purchased was not your everyday racing Alpine, but the actual championship car that both he and Carmichael had raced as half of a two-car, Alpine/Tiger team. Suddenly, Ellen felt better about the purchase.

As discovered, the Alpine's body was sound, probably due to the fact that it had been stored indoors from 1968 to 1998. The only previous damage had been on the car's right front fender, which had been hit by another Alpine when Carmichael was competing in the 1965 American Road Race of Champions. Silverstein decided to

Sessler was half of the official Rootes Group factory team. Sessler's car (right) was painted the same as Dan Carmichael's B-Production Sunbeam Tiger (left), who raced for the Sports Car Forum team of Columbus, Ohio. *Steve Silverstein*

refurbish the old race car rather than restore it, so instead of a new paint job, he used compound to bring luster back to the car's forty-year-old paint finish. The interior hasn't been changed: Armor-All was used on the original seats and tonneau cover and a thorough washing of the interior and floorpans cleansed thirty years of grime and achieved a certain patina that restored cars can never match.

The engine was a bit more of a challenge. Oilzum lubricant had gummed up the internals, requiring a thorough soaking to free up the pistons. In the process, Silverstein found that the engine block had been changed at some point from a standard 1600-cc engine to a replacement 1725-cc block. Interestingly, the cylinder head had once been modified by Joe Mondello, a renowned West Coast tuner usually associated with Oldsmobile V-8 drag racing engines.

Sunbeam Alpine No. 74 is now back on the track, as Silverstein often races the car in eastern vintage sports car events. I featured

When current owner Steve Silverstein purchased this clapped-out race car, he hoped to strip off the good parts for another Alpine restoration project. After some investigation, though, he discovered that he had actually purchased a significant race car. *Steve Silverstein*

With lots of elbow grease, Silverstein refurbished the Alpine, but utilized most of the original parts and even polished the original paint. *Steve Silverstein*

Silverstein in a March 2004 *Road & Track* magazine story about the Lime Rock Vintage Fall Festival. At Lime Rock, Silverstein is roughly 1.5 seconds slower than when original racer Sessler lapped the track at 1 minute, 13 seconds. But he told me he was having the best time of his life, and hoped that his lap times would get faster. Both car and driver epitomize what vintage racing is all about: racing famous and not-so-famous sports cars, but mostly about having fun.

Since his acquisition in 2000, Silverstein has accumulated a huge amount of documentation on his once semi-famous car, including race results, practice times, and preparation notes. The Sunbeam won both the 1964 National F-Production Championship with Sessler as driver, and the 1964 Divisional Championship with Carmichael driving. In the process, the car chalked up an impressive number of first- and second-place finishes by both Sessler (1964) and Carmichael (1964 to 1967).

Silverstein has also corresponded with both drivers, who are in their 70s. In fact, Sessler attended the Alpine Owners Club convention in 2001, where he was thrilled to once again be reunited with his car.

Rescuing an Allard

BY KRIS PALMER

Sydney Allard blazed a trail that many manufacturers—Shelby, Aston Martin, Facel Vega, Bristol, Rover, and others—would follow: he put an American V-8 in a British-built car. He started with flathead Fords because he owned a Ford dealership in England. But the car really took off, from the starting line and in the public eye, when he installed a Cadillac V-8. The Allard was a serious performance machine that struck fear into the hearts of much larger, older, better-funded competitors.

Motorsports enthusiasts in the United States took notice and placed orders. They could not buy complete cars, however, unless perhaps they wanted flathead-Ford power. Other V-8 powerplants were not available after the war because of England's trade policy. The country wanted goods going out and cash coming it. It would not allow Allard to buy and import American engines. Instead, U.S. buyers would tell Sydney which engine they planned to fit when the car came across the Atlantic. His shop would then outfit the chassis with the engine mounts and radiator to suit.

This Allard J2X was stored in a tractor-trailer storage box for more than thirty years. Much of the body damage was caused because a race car was hung by chains above the Allard, and each time the box was moved the Allard was damaged.
David Watson

Allards raced at the top of the game until the bigger manufacturers caught up, and they continued to hold their own for years afterward in other racing venues. Today they are seldom seen and highly prized.

David Watson's 1952 Allard J2X was one of only eighty-five produced. Its third owner raced it on the East Coast in the 1950s and sold it to a forgotten buyer. A seventeen-year-old got hold of it sometime thereafter and raced it around on his family's farm in Titusville, New Jersey. In 1965, another New Jersey man bought the car and stowed it away. He liked to buy sports cars in need of repair and always planned to fix them. But while he often got around to the buying, he rarely managed to do the fixing.

Because of this habit, the New Jersey man's property was scattered with classic British sports cars—Jaguars, Healeys, MGs, and others. Local residents were aware of the collection and hopeful buyers would often turn up at his door. Yet he refused their offers because he planned to fix them. Still, no fixing occurred.

Rumors of the cars found their way to Connecticut, to a dealer in collector automobiles. This prospective buyer had the winning plan: he offered to buy all the cars, and this collective sum had the power to change the owner's perspective. He accepted, and the buyer immediately phoned every wrecker and towing service within forty miles to come and haul the cars away before anyone got cold feet.

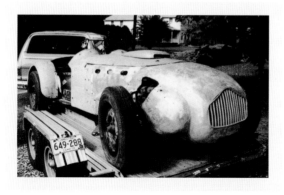

Once the car was pushed out of the storage box and onto a trailer, its new owner, David Watson, was able to assess his purchase. Even though the aluminum body was badly dented, the car had been stored out of the weather, so it was basically sound. *David Watson*

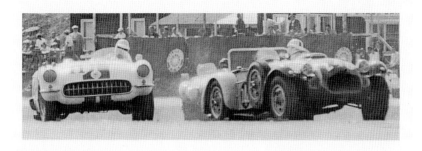

Watson's Allard J2X as a race car in the late 1950s. It wore the number 246 and raced with knock-off Halibrand magnesium wheels. *David Watson*

Among the many cars lying about the property was a tractor-trailer box serving as a storage barn. Not surprisingly, that storage was devoted to cars. What was surprising, though, were the cars that were hidden, and the curious manner in which they were held. Suspended from a chain in the ceiling was a race car. Below it was a classic roadster. What type of roadster was hard to determine because the lower car had taken quite a beating. The property owner would occasionally move the trailer, and when he did, the race car would bounce around and wallop the car below. Unlike the cars outside, this one was protected from the elements. Yet the cars parked outside didn't have another car bouncing around on top of them.

The lower car was a 1952 Allard J2X, which turned up in *Hemmings* and on eBay. It was the rarest car on the property, and David Watson was the lucky buyer—lucky being a matter of perspective. The engine was wrong for the car and when Watson removed the manual transmission, he found a Hydramatic flexplate bolted to the crankshaft. The rear end was also wrong, and many other parts were incorrect or missing.

Watson spent a few months gathering parts and finding the correct engine—a 331-cubic-inch Cadillac V-8—and getting it worked on. He had a chassis shop fit a correct rear end. At that point, he had a rolling chassis and a horrible body with an engine in it. He loaded it onto a trailer and took it to Barry Parker's restoration shop.

The Allard begins to take shape in Watson's Pennsylvania garage. The body was widened by two inches during restoration to accommodate safety rear hubs and alloy wheels so it could be driven in vintage racing events. *David Watson*

When other Allard enthusiasts saw the car, their impressions were cautious at best. The consensus seemed to be that Watson's J2X was damaged beyond repair. Watson and Parker had a different view.

Parker worked on the J2X continually, allowing Watson to perform mechanical work in the shop at the same time. In nine months the two men had the car in drivable condition, and in one year the car was done. When the Allard club saw the finished car, it gave Watson the Lazarus Award for raising it from the dead. Watson duly thanked Parker for his tireless and remarkable efforts.

In the five or six years Watson has owned the car, he has learned much of its history. During its racing years, the car made the motoring press and was featured in photographs in various race programs. Some of the car's features and modifications, including a hole in the cowling to permit side exhaust, helped Watson identify it from these old photos, and tracking down the individuals named confirmed the car's identity.

Watson drives his freshly restored Allard as he competes in the Hershey Hillclimb in May 2005. Note that the car is wearing the number 246, as it did when it raced in the 1950s. The car also won Best in Show at the Carlisle (Pennsylvania) British car meet in September 2004. *David Watson*

As Watson notes, "When you have only eighty-five cars total, it's not too hard to put it together." Chassis No. 2222 (not tied to the number produced) was delivered to the United States in January 1952, and Watson has photos of it dating back to July of that year.

Watson's car no longer sits hidden as it did for so many years. He's taken the car to Watkins Glen, as well as events in Pittsburgh and Texas. He goes to all of the Allard gatherings, trailering the car. But it's a driver too, and when the sun shines he and his wife take it out for summer drives and errands. They also take it to car gatherings around their home in central Pennsylvania, where there's something almost every weekend throughout the summer.

Found and restored at last, the J2X is a keeper. Watson plans to hold on to it and enjoy it.

The Missing Lightweight

Hidden deep inside a California garage sat a long-buried time capsule. This treasure, a rare aluminum Jaguar E-Type, had been there for more than three decades and was still undiscovered, even though scores of Jaguar collectors from around the world had been searching for the "missing lightweight." Yes, the racer eluded even the most diligent car hunters. And it's pretty safe to assume that if its eccentric owner, Howard Gidovlenko, hadn't died the famous race car would still be hidden.

Four decades before Gidovlenko's car was unearthed, the first two Lightweight E-Types, No. S850660 and No. S850659, were rushed through production in order to compete in the Sebring twelve-hour race in March 1963. The former car is now recognized as the first production lightweight. It was sold to Briggs Cunningham and entered at Sebring for drivers Bruce McLaren and Walt Hansgen. The second Jag (and the subject of this story) was sold to the company's West Coast importer, Kjell Qvale, for $5,000 on October 29, 1963.

The cars were eventually flown from England to Miami and transported to the track. There was a problem, though: *both* cars carried the Cunningham racing colors of white with blue stripes. Thanks to some quick thinking and a can of red paint found in a Sebring hanger, Qvale's car soon looked different from the other Jag.

The cars were visually identical to their E-Type street brethren. Except for the drivetrain, which consisted of a 315-horsepower dry sump, injected 3.8-liter aluminum engine, and five-speed ZF gearbox, they were very close to stock.

Qvale's car was driven by Ed Leslie and Frank Morrill to a seventh-place overall finish with 195 laps completed—fourteen laps less than the winning Ferrari 250P, but first in class and one position higher than Cunningham's car. Leslie's and Morrill's Sebring performance proved to be the best of any of the lightweights in a top-level long-distance event.

This rare and missing Jaguar Lightweight E-Type was discovered in a San Francisco garage. The car had only competed in two races—the 1963 Sebring twelve-hour event and a SCCA race at Laguna Seca before it was parked with only 2,663 miles on it. *John Mayston-Taylor*

At the conclusion of the Sebring race, Leslie drove the car—complete with racing livery, open exhaust, and a suitcase strapped to the trunk—back to Miami, where it was air freighted to San Francisco for its next race in June. The race was held at Laguna Seca, and was the third round of SCCA's United States Road Racing Championship series. This time Leslie drove the car solo, where he finished eighth. (Chuck Parsons won the race in a Lotus 23.)

After the Laguna Seca race, Qvale had the Jag transported to his dealership in San Francisco. It remained there until October, when it was purchased by World War II decorated RAF flying ace Gidovlenko. He bought the car for $5,000 at the financed rate of $143.83 per month. His intention was to begin campaigning the Jag at the 1964 24 Hours of Daytona, and he began preparing for the season by purchasing numerous spare parts from the factory. Included in the parts were three new sets of Dunlop lightweight wheels, a set of new tires, camshaft blanks, brake sets, and spare clutches.

Gidovlenko also began modifying the car based on his knowledge of aircraft technology. He used boxed sections of aluminum to brace and strengthen the Jag's shell, and he treated the car's exposed aluminum interior panels with zinc chromate, an etching primer. Then, after dropping the rear suspension, removing the engine, and covering the body with a film of oil, he put the car into an owner-induced coma for the next thirty-five years. In fact, there's no record of Gidovlenko ever driving the car. When it was discovered on February 28, 1998, the 1963 license tags were unused.

When Gidovlenko died, his family was clearing out his personal effects at his house in early 1988 and family members eventually made it to the two garages. "In the second garage—the one at the end of the garden—they began to go through the pile of empty cardboard boxes that actually covered the Jag," says John Mayston-Taylor, chairman of Lynx Motors, who ultimately purchased the car for a private collector. "At first they believed it was simply an old E-Type, but when they posted details of the car on the Internet, they were besieged by dealers, brokers, and opportunists from around the world who tried to convince Gidovlenko's heirs they would take if off their hands for a fraction of its value."

Gidovlenko's executor, Denis Darger, a retired Los Angeles narcotics policeman, decided it would be best to consult Jaguar expert Terry Larson. His family agreed that since the car was the major part of Gidovlenko's estate, it should be auctioned off to get the best price for it. RM Auction in Monterey, California, was given the task of hosting the event.

Interest in the car, of course, was very high, especially because the Jag only had a mere 2,663 miles on its odometer, meaning that the car had traveled further by airplane—first from England to Florida, then to San Francisco—than it ever traveled on its wheels!

The car also had a great history. Jaguar had committed to build a dedicated competition version of its new E-Type after it competed successfully against the likes of the Ferrari 250 GTO in 1961. The factory first made a light, steel-bodied version, but no records have been found to show that the car was actually raced. The factory then built eleven aluminum-bodied lightweight roadsters for the 1963 season to compete in the GT World Championship. By that time, Enzo Ferrari realized the E-Type's promise and constructed the "Jag Beater"—the all-conquering GTO—in response.

Rather than campaigning the cars itself, Jaguar sold the lightweights to privateers who entered them in races across Europe, Australia, Africa, and the United States—where they faced stiff competition from Ferraris and Cobras. Before Gidovlenko's family uncovered No. S850660, all of the other lightweights had been accounted for, leaving this car as the mystery enthusiasts dubbed "the missing lightweight."

While the car had been virtually untouched for years, it did have rough patches of bare aluminum on its body, which didn't seem to fit with the meticulous manner in which Gidovlenko had stored his prized Jag. Later on, family members concluded that the patches were apparently created during a divorce settlement, when the owner purposely roughed up the car in order to reduce its perceived value.

Fast forward thirty-plus years: the Jaguar indeed proved to be a good investment, rough patches and all. Mayston-Taylor bought it with an $872,050 bid on behalf of an anonymous client. Not a bad bit of appreciation, considering the car's original bill states that Qvale purchased the car as a demonstrator on October 29, 1963, for $5,000.

The plan was for the car to be spirited off to the Lynx shops in Hastings, England, for analysis and resurrection, but U.S. authorities made things more difficult by refusing to believe that an E-Type could be worth so much money. They suspected a money laundering scheme. Eventually, the car was finally released and loaded onto a 747 cargo jet (transported by air yet again!) to be shipped to Lynx.

The new owner planned to preserve the car's originality, but after a thorough inspection at Lynx he decided to refurbish rather than restore. The car would not be repainted; instead, Lynx would carefully blend new paint with the original paint to refinish the hood, doors, and rear bodywork that had been scuffed to the bare aluminum during Gidovlenko's divorce. The original paint had faded to three different tints, so a custom blend of the three colors was "soft-masked" and blown in.

The Jag's suspension was dismantled and crack-checked, which surprisingly revealed stress fractures from just the two races. The car's structure was further reinforced in the area of the roll bar, where strengthening plates were inserted. Additionally, a modern fuel cell was inserted inside the original gas tank.

Nearly all the original engine parts were reused, including the connecting rods, piston rings, cams, and valves. Only the head studs, the water pump impeller, and bearings were renewed.

Additionally, two gauges were added. One gauge would record fuel pressure (below 100 psi could burn a piston), and the other gauge would be for engine oil temperature.

The car had more body damage than anyone could remember. Those familiar with the car suspected that the previous owner attempted to devalue it during a divorce settlement by scratching up the paint. *John Mayston-Taylor*

The Jag's rejuvenation took only three months—incredible, considering that it was disassembled down to the smallest detail. When completed, the car was shaken down at Goodwood in the capable hands of professional road racer Andy Wallace. Wallace had won the 24 Hours of Le Mans driving a Jaguar XJR in 1988.

The car's new owner wanted it to compete on the same circuits it had in 1963, so in March 1999, it was entered in the Sebring vintage races wearing the same No. 23 that it had worn there thirty-six years prior. Even though this car was "vintage" in every sense of the word compared to more modernized vintage cars, driver Mayston-Taylor

Back on the track after so many years. The Lightweight E-Type shows off its recent restoration by owner John Mayston-Taylor's Lynx Motors. It eventually entered in the Sebring historic races and the Monterey historics, at the two tracks it had competed on forty years earlier. *John Mayston-Taylor*

149

finished remarkably well: third overall and first in class. In September 1999, the car was shipped to San Francisco where it competed in the Monterey historic races, its second race at that circuit in thirty-six years. One interested spectator was the car's original driver, Ed Leslie, who recently passed away, but was then a resident of nearby Carmel. Leslie rode as a passenger in parade laps as an emotional Mayston-Taylor loped around the Laguna Seca circuit with the man who piloted this very car during another time.

During the race, Mayston-Taylor was again impressive, finishing twelfth overall behind the V-8 muscle of Shelbys, Cobras, and Corvettes.

So ends an amazing story about an amazing car that literally came full circle.

CHAPTER SIX

"Professional" Car Hunters

A Car Hunter's Tale

BY BILL WARNER

Although I am known among some car people as a photographer for *Road & Track* magazine, I had to make a real living as a purveyor of industrial filtration equipment. I spent my days traveling the southeastern states and hoping someone would buy my wares so that I could support my car habit. As a traveling salesman, you have some choices to make during the off hours in strange cities along the way: *1)* You can end up in a bar drinking every evening and become an alcoholic . . . or worse, or *2)* You can scavenge junkyards and repair shops looking for old cars.

151

I have been luckier than most and have stumbled across a number of really neat cars that I have restored (or had restored). To be honest, my investments in these cars have been very beneficial for the most part. The following are the most interesting of these finds:

1964 TEAM ELITE/SID TAYLOR (EX–DENNY HULME, FRANK GARDNER) BRABHAM BT8

I was in Columbia, South Carolina, in 1976, perusing my favorite newsstand for some on-the-road reading, when I ran into an old friend, Rex Davis. We got into a discussion on "Birdcage" Maseratis and how I always wanted one to restore. Rex mentioned that there was one in an imported car scrapyard in Columbia, and ten minutes later we were there. The proprietor, Bill Broome, advised that it wasn't a Typo 60/61 "Birdcage," but a 450S, and he had sold it several years ago. I asked if he had any other old race cars lying around, to which he replied that he had an ex–Denny Hulme Brabham. Thinking it was a formula car, I wasn't too interested.

Once we got to his storage area, I was pleased to see it was, in fact, a BT8, two-liter, sports racer. It was one of twelve built, serial No. SC6-64, and it was the sixth car built by Jack Brabham and Ron Tauranac in 1964. The car was complete, with the exception of the starter motor, windshield, headlights, and headlight covers. Amazingly, it had the original ignition key, HD-5 gearbox, and two-liter FPF engine.

The car had a blown head gasket and had not run in some time, though. It had flared rear fenders with oversize slicks, but all in all, it was in pretty good shape. We struck a deal at $3,000, which was a princely sum for an old race car in 1976. You've got to remember that there was no vintage racing in the East, and Steve Earle was just getting started on the West Coast. Still, I felt that vintage racing was a growth area in motorsports.

I paid for the car, borrowed a trailer, hooked it up to my wife's brand-new Olds wagon, and then brought the car back to my home in Jacksonville. Several weeks later, I was at Sebring when Team

While searching in a Columbia, South Carolina, junkyard for a "Birdcage" Maserati in 1976, Bill Warner discovered this ex–Denny Hulme Brabham BT8 in the same yard. The car, No. SC6-64, was the sixth of twelve built and was complete, including the original ignition key! Warner paid the princely sum of $3,000 and dragged it home on a borrowed trailer. *Bill Warner*

McLaren's Spanky Smith introduced me to Colin Day. Day was an English fabricator who, among many things, had been the wrench on Peter Revson's very successful BT8 (owned by Bill Kay of Poughkeepsie). Colin was looking for work, and I needed someone who knew race cars to restore this one, my first foray into collector cars.

One thing I learned early on was to research the car completely prior to undertaking the restoration and to proceed with kid gloves. Gently sanding the doors with 600-grit waterproof sandpaper, I uncovered the names "Geoff Breakell" and "Harold Day." Yet "Team Elite" or "Denny Hulme" did not appear. With the help of my friend, the great driver Brian Redman, I contacted Geoff Breakell. Geoff informed me that he had bought the car from Sid Taylor. Bingo!! With a lot of research in the *Road & Track* files, my own records, and thorough conversations with David Hobbs, David Piper, Sid Taylor, and Geoff Breakell, I pieced together the car's history.

It was owned originally by Team Elite and driven by Frank Gardner. Frank ran the car at Riverside and Laguna Seca in 1965.

Afterward, it was sold to Sid Taylor for Denny Hulme. In 1966, it was undefeated in the under-two-liter class throughout the season, winning the Tourist Trophy outright at Oulton Park (upsetting David Hobbs in the new Lola T70). It was arguably the most successful under-two-liter car of the 1960s.

Later, as I dug through old British magazines that I had picked up from Bruce Perry of the Yellow Dog Garage, I found out more. The car had run a street race in Morocco, leading Piper in the Ferrari 250P and Jo Schlesser in a 427 Cobra until mechanical problems sidelined it. So, out of a South Carolina junkyard came an absolutely marvelous race car, a car with impeccable provenance, good looks, and no bad habits. I raced it from 1977 to 1989, when I reluctantly sold it for business reasons. But boy, was it a great racer . . . very fast and very forgiving. It is the one car I wish that I had kept.

1964 LANG COOPER (KING COOPER)

In 1977, I received a call from Bill Broome in Columbia asking if I would be interested in a Cooper Ford. I knew that most (but not all) Cooper Fords were built by Carroll Shelby, so I was indeed interested. When I arrived at the scrapyard/service shop that was Broome's Garage, I found an engineless race car in scruffy, mostly bare aluminum with a crude wing lying on the back deck. I did not recognize the car right off the bat, but I shot a few photos and aired them out to John Dinkel at *Road & Track*.

John called back immediately and suggested that I buy the car. It was the last of the Cooper Fords (King Cobras) built by Shelby, with a body by Don Edmunds and a design by Peter Brock. It was built for Craig Lang, heir to the Olympia Beer fortune, hence, the "Lang" Cooper name. The correct engine for the car was a five-bolt Ford 289, and fortunately the Quad Weber carburetor setup and intake manifold were still with the car.

I located a correct engine, and my friend Jack Roush built me a fantastic race motor. Then one of the most talented aluminum men in the business, Wayne Sparling, repaired the bodywork and the late

One year after discovering the Brabham, Warner returned to the same South Carolina junkyard to discover this Lang Cooper Ford, a.k.a. the King Cobra. The car was designed in 1964 by Peter Brock and built by Carroll Shelby to compete in the early USRRC and Can-Am races. *Bill Warner*

With the bodywork removed, the Lang Cooper chassis shows that it was all business. The car was powered by a five-bolt 289 engine, Weber carbs and manifold, and Collotti gearbox, and it scared everyone who drove it. *Bill Warner*

Freshly restored, the Lang Cooper (foreground) and the Brabham BT8 make a handsome pair. Warner discovered that the two had actually raced each other on two occasions—at Laguna Seca and Riverside—in the 1960s. *Bill Warner*

Alf Francis rebuilt the Collotti/Frances gearbox. Peter Brock helped me with the correct paint and design details; Dave Friedman provided the historical photos; Al Dowd at Shelby's took care of the details; and the original builder, Wally Peat, managed the suspension and other chassis details.

My years with *Road & Track* paid great dividends. Strangely, the photos from Friedman illustrated a spooky fact: the Brabham I had bought a year earlier from Broome had raced against the Lang Cooper at Laguna and Riverside. To make matters even spookier, he sent me a shot of the two cars side by side at Riverside. Sometimes truth is stranger than fiction. Colin Day restored the car and I took it to Sebring in about 1980.

I chose Sebring because the runways are really wide and if something goes wrong, you have a long way to go before you hit something substantial. As I entered the back straightaway, I came up on my pal Bill Ferran in his 2.5 Carrera. I squeezed the power on and rocketed by him as if I was tethered to a space shuttle. I noticed that the nose came up and the steering got very, very, very light. The car had abominable handling and aerodynamics. I called it quits after thirty minutes. I took it to Taimiami next, and then to SAAC 11. Then I called the original driver, Ed Leslie, and mentioned that I had finally finished the restoration and had driven it. "How'd you like it?" he asked. "Scared me to death," I answered. "Me, too," he responded.

I restored the car as it appeared on the cover of the April 1964 *Sports Car Graphic*—which, though correct, was not particularly prudent as it needed canards and spoilers to make it even reasonably stable. Though it was one of the most beautiful racers of the mid-1960s (Ruskit even made a slot car model of it), the ride left too much to be desired, so I sold it in 1990.

1971 GROUP 44 TRIUMPH TR6
(EX–BOB TULLIUS, JOHN MCCOMB, PAUL NEWMAN)

Tommy Ciccone, one of our team drivers in a Firehawk race at Watkins Glen, knew that I was a vintage race car fan, so when he wanted to sell his ex–Paul Newman, D-Production National Championship Triumph TR6, he knew who to call.

The car had not been raced in years. It came with three of everything—wheels, gearboxes, diffs, body panels, and a slew of other spares. The price was reasonable, but it was 1990 and there was not a class in which to run a 1971 production car. Still, I bought it sight unseen, and had a friend of mine pick it up—it had been in a garage in Watkins Glen all along.

The funny part was that it was in a garage less than a quarter-mile from Vic Francese, owner of the Glen Motor Lodge. Vic is one of the great early vintage racers with a McLaren and an early Aston. And here was this two-time national championship racer sitting just down the hill from his establishment. The first time he ever saw it during the nine years it had been in the Glen was the day they loaded it on the trailer to haul it to me. Boy, was he ever ticked! He called me on the phone to "jokingly" say that I was stealing the car

One that got away. Warner chased down this Lola T70 Mk. III in Panama City, Florida, which was for sale in 1978 for $1,500. But when the seller raised the price to $4,000 after Warner arrived, Warner called the deal off. In retrospect, even though it was missing the engine, gearbox, gauges, calipers, and steering wheel, he wishes he had bought it. *Bill Warner*

from him. Of course, I told him "jokingly" that I had already given him nine years to find it.

The car arrived in the silver-and-black Paul Newman livery, but I chose to restore it back to Group 44 white with green wheels and nose stripe. Brian Fuerstenau, who originally built the car at Group 44, did the engines and gearboxes, and Colin Day did all the rest with the help of Brian, Lanky Foushee, and Bob Tullius. The car was an acid-dipped, full-blown race car with too many tricks to list here. After a one-year restoration, I took the car to Savannah where I won the one-hour enduro by whipping up on Corvettes, Porsche 911s, a lone Lotus 23, and about twenty other vintage racers. Even today,

Wouldn't you know it: Warner stumbles across one of the most famous race cars of the past thirty years in a garage outside of Watkins Glen, New York. The Group 44 TR6 won two national SCCA D-Production Championships—one with John McComb and the other with Paul Newman. Here it is restored with Group 44 founder Bob Tullius and chief mechanic Brian Fuerstenau. They are standing in front of Tullius' restored P-51. *Bill Warner*

thirty-one years after it first raced, it is still a force to be reckoned with on short- and medium-speed courses (such as Lime Rock, Barbers, Savannah, and Summit Point). Daytona and Road Atlanta are a little long for the limited horsepower (between 210 and 220), but I take great pride in having lapped Lime Rock at 1:00.4.

It is a wonderful car to drive; it's very balanced, quick, and strong. It sounds amazing when a great meaty sound blasts out of its twin megaphone exhausts. It is a car that goes about as fast as I want to go, and it feels comfortable, like an old shoe. I like nothing better than beating up 911s, Shelbys, and small-block Corvettes with it, just like Tullius, Newman, and McComb used to do. It is, arguably, the best production racer of the early 1970s, and I love every minute I am in it.

1956 Ex-Works Lotus 11 Le Mans, No. 209

When you get a reputation for buying old race cars, you don't have to find them. They eventually find you. One day I received a call from a friend, Jerry Rehkopf, that went something like this: "You like old race cars, right? Well, go out to Harry's Towing on U.S. 1. They just hauled an old Jaguar race car out of a garage on Girvan Road."

Girvan Road was about five miles from my house, not far from Brumos Porsche, and the last place I would have looked for a race car. It seems the lady who had the car was going to a retirement home and called Harry to haul it and a couple of old Lincolns away. The Lotus had belonged to her late husband, but how it got to Jacksonville was and is unknown. The nice thing about old cars is that they have wheels and can show up just about anywhere.

It took me about ten minutes to get to Harry's, where his wife took me out back to see the car. "What kind of Jaguar is it?" she asked. "It's a Lotus kind of Jaguar," I said. "Is it worth something?" she further queried. "A bucket of manure is worth something to a farmer."

Warner was embarrassed when this Lotus 11 was uncovered in a backyard just a few miles from his home in Jacksonville, Florida. When the local towing guy said he just dragged in "some kind of Jaguar," Warner couldn't believe it. Then the towing guy did some further investigating and the "Jaguar" . . . er, Lotus, quickly jumped in value from $2,500 to $12,000. Warner bought it anyway. *Bill Warner*

A couple of years' worth of elbow grease and the Lotus was in concours condition. Here former champion race driver Brian Redman tests the car for a *Road & Track* magazine salon feature. Today the car sits in the Barber Motorsports Museum in Birmingham, Alabama. *Bill Warner*

I asked her what they planned to do with it and she said that Harry was going to put a small-block Chevy in it for her to drive. I explained that the Chevy would be a bit much for the chassis. Because the engine was missing, I explained that I would be more interested in the car if it had the original engine. Harry went back to the garage and retrieved the original engine, stored in about three boxes. The block was warped from many repairs, but it was complete.

I made the mistake of offering too little for it, $2,500, and before I knew it, Harry had shopped it around. Soon the price had risen to $12,000. I called Brian Redman and he suggested that $12,000 was a good price, so Harry and I struck a deal. At the time, a good price for a restored Lotus was about $90,000 to $100,000, so $12,000 really was not too unreasonable.

I called Innes Ireland, who I had driven with at Nelson Ledges in a Jack Roush SVO Mustang and had worked with on a number of *Road & Track* projects, and he connected me to Vic Thomas of the Lotus 11 registry. When I mentioned that I had found Lotus 11 No. 209, Thomas told me that there were at least two Loti running around the UK claiming to be No. 209. It seems that when a significant car disappears for a long time, there are a number of less-than-honest souls who will clone it for their own benefit.

Vic would not give me any history on it until he was convinced that I had the real car. Thankfully, photos of the builder's plate and of the car and the engine block serial numbers were enough to convince him that the car in Jacksonville was indeed the real No. 209. We still did not know much about the car, though, other than it was a works Le Mans and that Nos. 210, 211, and 212 were the team Le Mans cars.

You need big names attached to the history of a car, so I called it the ex–Pope Paul/Elvis Presley Lotus 11, two of the biggest names I could come up with. For a while, I thought it was a Cliff Allison car, and that he may have driven it at some time when it was in factory hands. However, later records showed that it belonged to Mike Clarke and was, in fact, driven by Innes Ireland.

For the restoration, Colin Day did the chassis, Dick Greene did the aluminum work, and Bill Hutton of Hutton Engineering did the engine. When it was finished, Brian Redman and I did a salon in

Another one that got away: this was an odd combination of a 1938 Alfa Romeo 6C2300 chassis (complete with engine, gearbox, and suspension) mated with a customized Studebaker body. *Bill Warner*

What were they thinking? Who knows whatever happened to the original Alfa Romeo coachwork that was discarded in favor of this customized Studebaker body. Warner was unable to purchase the project. *Bill Warner*

Road & Track on the car. We restored it as an original Lotus 11 with the original fuel tank and no rollover bar. We did mount a pair of Webers in place of the SUs, along with Aeroquip brake and oil lines. I did a multipart report on restoring a vintage racer in *Vintage Motorsport* and sold the car shortly after finishing it to George Barber for his museum in Birmingham. It was a very nice car, but a little small for me to race. It was an original car as well, and I didn't want to screw it up by converting it to a current racer. I'm glad George now has it in his significant Lotus collection.

1934 FORD MODEL 40 SPECIAL SPEEDSTER (EDSEL FORD'S SPORTS CAR)

Of all the cars I've been fortunate enough to find, the 1934 Ford Model 40 Special Speedster has to be the most significant. The car was designed in 1934 by Ford's first design chief, E. T. "Bob" Gregorie, for Henry Ford's son, Edsel. It is known as the Continental Series II car because Edsel coined its look as "continental." It is, in

Another terrific barn find! Warner discovered one of the most sought-after early Fords in history in a DeLand, Florida, carport. It was Edsel Ford's hot rod—the Model 40 Special Speedster. The aluminum two-seater was built for Henry Ford's son by Ford Aircraft in 1934. After uncovering it from decades worth of rubbish, Warner discovered a sound car, so here it is, basically unrestored. *Bill Warner*

fact, the second car in a series of three; the third car was the original 1939 Lincoln Continental.

The car remained with Edsel from 1934 until his death in 1943. It was then sold and ended up at Coachcraft in California. In *Road & Track*'s third issue in 1948, it was advertised for $2,500. The car then came east and was purchased in 1959 by a young sailor, John Pallasch, for $603 off a used car lot in Pensacola, Florida. Shortly after he purchased the car, it threw a fan belt and its engine cooked. Then, from sometime in 1960 until I bought the car in 1999, it sat idle in a DeLand, Florida, garage.

I had been aware of the car for about twenty years, but I did not know who owned it. While judging at Meadow Brook with the great automotive historian Michael Lamm, I remembered that he had written an article for *Special Interest Autos* on the car. He had recalled that the owner's name was Pallasch. Upon returning to Jacksonville, I loaded my address CD into my computer and scanned for a Pallasch in the DeLand area. I found him in nearby

Orange City. I called, not so much to buy the car, but to invite him to show the car at The Amelia Island Concours d'Elegance, of which I am founder and chairman. He told me, "I don't want to show the damn thing. It hasn't run in about forty years. I want to sell it." An hour later, I was in DeLand negotiating to buy the car. It took two more visits and help from my friend Jack Boxstrom, but I finally closed the deal.

The car had been stuffed in the back corner of Pallasch's garage. To prevent his neighbors from seeing the car when the garage door was open, he had piled grocery bags full of aluminum cans around and on top of it. As he unpiled the bags and unveiled the car, I felt like Indiana Jones in the *Temple of Doom*. Here was one of the most significant Fords of all time—Edsel Ford's personal sports car, unrestored with a blown engine and a cheap paint job, and basically unmolested.

Back in Jacksonville, I did an inventory of "needs" and came up with few. The seats needed upholstering, the engine needed repair, the gas tank had forty-year-old fuel still in it, and the fenders were dinged and torn in a couple of areas. Other than that, it was in pretty good shape. A neighbor of mine who was into Fords came to see the car, and he said he had exactly what I needed—a new 1940 flathead V-8—still in the packing crate.

We unpacked my neighbor's engine, checked the bottom end, mounted the dual carburetors, ran an Aeroquip line to the carbs from a marine gas tank (we could not get the old tank out to clean it up—I left that to RM Restorations to handle), and the jewel fired on the second try. We repaired and repainted the fenders, touched up a few dents and scrapes, replaced the goofy-looking plexiglass wind-shields with proper glass ones, checked and repacked the bearings, checked the brakes, mounted a set of period double whitewalls from Corky Coker at Coker Tire Company, and showed the car at Amelia Island. Since then, the car has been shown at The Louis Vuitton Concours in New York City; Hershey, Pennsylvania; Meadow Brook, Michigan; and Hilton Head, South Carolina. It will run eighty-five miles per hour without a problem, and it elicits more thumbs-up than any other car I've ever owned.

In the course of finding these cars and others, I've learned a few things that I would like to pass on to fledgling ferrets:

1. If you are on a budget (and who isn't?), be knowledgeable and get excited over what you find. You may not find the car of your dreams, but you can work your way there through various other interesting cars.

2. Don't be in a hurry to start the restoration, but use your network to study the car before you dive in. In some cases, you may want to sell your discovery rather than restoring it. Restoring a car is like skydiving. Once you start, the only option is to pull the rip cord, or in this case, write the checks. You are least likely to make a mistake if you do your homework up front.

3. Realize that, for most of us, economics dictate that you cannot keep them all. Enjoy the project, and remember that in order to avoid being upside down (having more money in the car than you can get for it), you make your profit when you buy, not when you sell. I've made money, lost money, and broke even on various cars over the years, but today's high restoration costs leave little margin for error.

4. Never, never pass up on a rumor. I missed the rolling chassis and engine of a 1937 Alfa Romeo 6C2300 MM (which had a custom 1950s Studebaker body on it) because I did not hop on the deal right away.

5. If you know the value, don't lose it because you fancy yourself a wheeler-dealer. In 1977, I lost a sure deal on a Porsche RS60 Spyder because I wanted to strike a better deal. I offered $12,500 and the seller wanted $13,500. I've kicked myself every day since.

Nothing beats finding a real jewel in a barn, a garage, under a tarp in someone's backyard, or in a junkyard, but don't lose perspective of just how much time and expense you may face once you've found the car of your dreams. *Bonne Chance*.

A Nose for Cobras

Some people are just better at certain tasks than others. Remember those guys in high school who could throw a football in a perfect spiral all the way to the end zone during football season, and then hit home runs in the spring? And no matter how hard you tried or how much you practiced, you couldn't come close to their performance?

Lynn Park of Pasadena, California, has a talent like that for finding Cobras. While the rest of us dream of stumbling across just one Cobra in a barn during our lifetime, Park has hit home run after home run, finding and purchasing the coveted and rare cars that were produced in Carroll Shelby's shops.

Park's love affair with Cobras goes back to his teenage years when he, as a hot-rod crazy youth, had a conversation with his sister's boyfriend, who loved sports cars. "He showed me the first copy of *Road & Track* magazine I had ever seen, and it had a Cobra on the cover," says Park, who has spent the last eight years of his retirement manufacturing and selling replacement Cobra wheels under the

CSX2307, the 307th 289 Cobra built, sat in a California backyard for more than a quarter-century. Even though the aluminum body was in sound condition, the leather interior and carpeting were terrible. *Tom Cotter*

The Cobra has one of the old black California license plates, which has been on the car for decades. *Tom Cotter*

name Trigo. "He said this new car was a hot rod *and* a sports car, and he joked that both of us could be happy with one."

Park's fire was lit. He jumped in his car the next day and tore off down the road to Venice, on the other side of Los Angeles, to see one for himself. It was love at first sight, but Park was just a high school teenager, and purchasing a new Cobra for more than $5,000 was out of the question. So he did the next best thing. He purchased an A.C. Aceca coupe and converted it to Cobra Dragon Snake specs. He purchased all the necessary parts directly from Shelby and built himself a hardtop version of the 289 Cobra. "I would talk Cobras all day long, but I couldn't afford a real one forty years ago," he says. "I'd spend every spare moment down at Shelby's shop. I had a friend who worked there, but I *lived* there!"

That passion became an obsession. Today, Park owns nine Cobras: seven 289 Cobras (CSX2010, 2044, 2176, 2259, 2307, 2364, and 2515) and two 427 Cobras (CSX3156 and 3203). He says he's on the lookout for one more because he'd like to have an even number of ten in his garage.*

*For a peek inside Park's garage, look at MBI Publishing Company's' *Ultimate Garages* by Phil Berg, page 129.

Another barn-find Cobra, the CSX2044, the 44th Cobra produced. Lynn Park purchased the car from its original owner, a rocket scientist from Stanford University. The car's history was well documented, including letters between the owner and Peter Brock of Shelby American. *Tom Cotter*

One of the interesting things about Park is that he's not restoration-oriented. Sure, a couple of his cars are in pristine condition, but he gets much more satisfaction from owning nonrestored "beater" Cobras. He prefers cars that can be driven on real road trips rather than cars that are moved from one garage to another inside enclosed trailers. For instance, every year Park and about a dozen of his friends take aggressive trips of 2,000 miles or more in their original Cobras. Often the owners refuse to erect the top or side curtains on their cars, despite the cold or rain. Clearly, these hearty folks don't look kindly upon owners who trailer their Cobras.

So even though Park has a couple of pristine show-quality Cobras in his collection, it's the as-found cars that he has the most interest in driving.

One car that Park is particularly fond of is CSX2307, affectionately referred to as "Dirt Bag." Lots of Cobra enthusiasts knew about the car that was covered with canvas in the Temple City,

California, backyard of the Charles Offenhauser family. These were relatives of Fred Offenhauser, who began manufacturing speed equipment for Model T, Model A, and Ford flathead V-8 engines in the 1930s. "It was just sitting there and wasn't for sale, even though guys with suitcases full of money would show up and attempt to buy the car. If Mrs. Offenhauser didn't like them, they didn't have a chance," Park says. "But a friend of mine finally talked them out of it. He bought it with the intention of converting it into a race car, but I bought it from him before he did anything to it. I convinced him that the car was so original and unmolested that it would be shame to cut it up."

It's not known how much the Offenhausers used the Cobra, but at some point, in about 1975, the car was parked in the backyard and covered with a tarp. When Park purchased CSX2307, it had 33,000 miles on the odometer. Since then he's put more than 2,000 additional miles on the car.

The car required lots of work. The gas tank needed a thorough cleaning, the carburetor needed to be rebuilt, and the fuel pump and water pump were changed. "Initially it smoked real bad, but I've run lots of Marvel Mystery Oil through it to loosen the piston rings, so now it doesn't smoke so badly anymore," he says. "My friends call it 'Dirt Bag.'"

The Shelby American World Registry lists CSX2307 as being delivered on March 20, 1964, to Sexton Ford Sales in Moline, Illinois. It was sold in red with black interior and white sidewall tires, radio, and antenna for the total sum of $5,734.55. By 1967, the car had found its way to a Los Angeles used car dealer, where it was purchased by Offenhauser. He had the car painted yellow and had the license plate "OFFIE" installed.

The car has a nonoriginal aluminum high-rise intake manifold and Holley carburetor, which may have been installed at the Ford dealer when new or by one of the subsequent owners. But the original engine No. 4067 remains in the car, and the original Goodyear Power Cushion 7.35-by-15 spare tire still resides in the trunk.

Because the CSX2044 was garaged, the interior is in nice, original condition. Park will keep the original paint, but rebuild the car's mechanical and hydraulic parts. *Tom Cotter*

The Cobra's interior was in terrible condition due to all of the years it was exposed to the elements. "There was lots of trash and mold in the cockpit," Park says. "I had to throw out the carpet because it was so rotten, and I used other seats because the leather and the seat frames were in awful condition." Additionally, the pedal assembly was frozen solid and required rebuilding. Despite all the rebuilding work, Park enjoys driving "Dirt Bag" more than any of his other Cobras. "People just go ape over this car," he says.

Another of Park's barn finds is Cobra CSX2044, the 44th Cobra produced by Shelby American. CSX2044 was invoiced to Shelby American on November 11, 1962, and sold to a Mr. Harrison "Hap" Horn of Palo Alto, California. Mr. Horn was eager to take delivery of his car, and he received a letter from Pete Brock of Shelby, updating him on its progress. "The paint looks great," said Brock of the white with red interior car. "The roll bar will be installed this afternoon, and may I suggest having it chromed instead of painting it, because we feel it just won't look right." Horn paid $7,297.33 for the well-optioned car and took delivery of it the following May. Because the car took a relatively long time to deliver, it came with a 289 engine instead of the 260-cubic-inch Ford that was in others with nearby serial numbers.

Horn drove the car just 22,000 miles before parking it in his garage in 1967. "The owner knocked off a muffler driving it into his garage and never drove it again," says Park, who adds that the car came complete with numerous letters between Horn and the Shelby organization. One letter from Horn asked why Cobras come equipped with generators instead of alternators. "Horn was a real rocket scientist—an aeronautics engineer at Stanford University," says Park, who purchased the car from Horn in 2001.

"Lots of guys knew about the car, but they all thought he [Horn] was asking too much money for it," Park adds. "But he was a gentleman and obviously a smart guy, so I bought it."

"I'm going to leave the original paint and interior, but I'm going to rebuild the mechanics and the engine; it has so much rust in the water jackets. The gas tank had eight or nine gallons of crystallized fuel in it when parked thirty years earlier, so cleaning out the fuel system was the messiest, smelliest job I've done on any car ."

According to Park, the engine turned over smoothly by hand, and he believes it would run, but because it sat for so many years with water in the cooling system, he'd rather not take any chances.

"I'm going to buff out the original paint; I think I can make it look pretty good," he says. "The original red carpets and seats are in incredible condition, so I'll use those as well."

Park was also on the trail of perhaps the most-prized Cobra of all time—CSX2287, the first Daytona Coupe—but he narrowly missed it. "I was so close to owning that car every step of the way," he laments.

The Automotive Archaeologist

Most auto enthusiasts would feel it quite an accomplishment to uncover two or three barn-find Porsches in their lifetime. But Steve Demosthenes, who sees himself as an "automotive archaeologist," has spent the better part of forty years pursuing and purchasing 356 series Porsches from hidden places all over the United States. He has uncovered more than 100 of the German sports cars, and even though the supply is drying up, he occasionally still discovers another one in a barn, or behind a fence.

His fascination with cars started early—not a surprise considering he grew up in the shadow of the Indianapolis 500 in the 1960s. "My first car was a souped-up '36 Ford sedan, followed by a '31 Ford with a Chevy engine, a '55 Chevy, a split-window '63 Corvette, and a 396-cubic-inch Sting Ray roadster," Demosthenes says. "All that power was intoxicating, but once I got a ride in my boss' sports car—a '58 Porsche Speedster, at age sixteen—it left an impression that never faded."

One of Steve Demosthenes' barn finds in 1970. Inspecting the car is one of his favorite traveling companions, a Great Dane named Tara. Demosthenes spent several years traveling the United States buying Porsche 356s, driving them to California, and selling them. *Steve Demosthenes*

Demosthenes posted ads like this in *Auto Trader* magazines around the country, and they became the best source of Porsche leads. *Steve Demosthenes*

WANTED PORSCHE SPEEDSTER
Or open 356 Porsche. Private party. Will consider any condition. Reasonably priced 1950 to 1965. Call if you have or know of one. Stephen. PH. Keywest, FL   *1/8-17/23*

"I remember it to this day: it was white, and it was the only Porsche I've ever seen with Daytona knock-off wire wheels."

Just a few years later, Demosthenes got his own sports car, an Austin-Healey "Bugeye" Sprite, but in 1968 he decided to buy a more practical sports car, so he narrowed his choices down to an Alfa Romeo and a Porsche 356.

"They were both in my price range, so don't ask me why, but I bought the Porsche. I eventually sold that Porsche and bought another and another, never with the intention of making a profit, but just for the opportunity to drive a variety of cars," he says.

By 1970, he was living in Los Angeles and had hooked up with a fellow Porsche fan from Baltimore. "He had a little bit of money, so I convinced him that we should fly to the Midwest, buy Porsches, and then drive them back to California to sell," Demosthenes says, adding that while Porsches weren't in demand in the Midwest, a willing buyer could always be found on the West Coast.

These were the days prior to the Internet, so Demosthenes relied heavily on the *Auto Trader* newspaper to find the cars. "I placed hundreds of want ads with a photo of an old Porsche to grab attention. When the *Auto Trader* went national, I hit the mother lode."

One of his best discoveries came after Demosthenes got a call from a guy in Brunswick, Georgia, responding to an *Auto Trader* ad. The caller mentioned that his recently deceased father had been a Porsche restorer and now those cars and parts needed to be sold. "I told him I was interested and drove up to see what he had," Demosthenes says. "Way back in the woods and down this country road, there was a strange-looking concrete structure with some totally rusted out body shells and a wonderfully original silver 1954 Continental Cabriolet. I immediately bought the car and had it trucked away to a friend's shop in Jacksonville, Florida." But the seller was very evasive about the possibility of the others being available for purchase.

Weeks later, after many phone calls, Demosthenes coerced the seller into showing him the other cars and parts, and that visit uncovered six or seven Porsches and tons of new old stock parts. Another deal was struck and Demosthenes began hauling the cars out. "On my last trip with the trailer, as we were loading parts, my girlfriend and I walked out of the garage to face several federal agents with their guns drawn," Demosthenes says with a laugh. "Turns out the cars didn't belong to his father, but instead to his ex-drug dealing partner who was wanted for murder and was on the run.

"So I had to return the Continental Cabriolet and all the other cars. I don't know what ever happened to the cars. I wound up losing about $5,000 on the deal. But losing that '54 Cabriolet was a heartbreaker."

Demosthenes loads one of the "drug cars" onto his trailer. He didn't realize the seller was the target of a Drug Enforcement Agency sting operation. He simply thought he was the lucky guy who was buying a bunch of old Porsches and parts. *Steve Demosthenes*

Another one of the cars Demosthenes attempted to buy from a man who was actually a drug dealer. Demosthenes thought he was purchasing six or seven 356 Porsches, but instead he and his girlfriend were temporarily arrested and questioned, then released. He had to return the cars and lost $5,000. *Steve Demosthenes*

Another barn-find story sparked by a 1991 *Auto Trader* want ad revolves around a 356 a guy knew about in eastern Washington state. "He told me about another 'old guy', Paul, who had a 356 sitting behind his garage," Demosthenes says. "So we drove to the location and met the owner. He showed us a very rusty, ratty 'A' coupe that was sitting outside."

In those days, cars like this were only considered as parts cars, so Demosthenes wasn't very interested in it. Then the "old guy" told him he had another Porsche in the garage.

Carefully navigating the yard littered with old lawn mowers, a crashed airplane, and assorted Porsche parts, they got to the garage, where Demosthenes could see a roof profile of a coupe from under boxes and years of discarded junk. Upon closer investigation, he found that the car's rear clip had been cut off and it had a considerable number of inner body panels that needed repair. It also had some holes cut out of the driver's side rear inner fender well, which he asked the owner about.

"Oh, all the Carreras had those for the oil cooler." the owner said.

Of course, the mention of the word Carrera made Demosthenes' heart rate almost double. "But I fought to show no interest or enthusiasm," he says. "I continued to keep the conversation flowing, still not fully convinced. I asked him where the engine was. He said, 'Oh, it's in the house.' He then showed me the cowl that covers the generator: it was unmistakably Carrera."

"But would he sell? NO!"

For the next thirteen years, Demosthenes continued to contact Paul about the car—even making the 150-mile drive to visit—but the answer was always no. But finally, in 2004, Demosthenes convinced the owner to sell the Carrera four-cam engine in exchange for a freshly rebuilt 356 engine, which he loaded into his truck and drove to Paul's.

"After thirteen years, I finally saw the four-cam engine hanging from a hoist in his guest bedroom, surrounded by old newspapers and trash; it had been placed there in 1969. The Carerra engine was finally mine," Demosthenes says. "I went back to see him

This is Porsche No. 5047, which was built in August 1950. It was the 38th Porsche 356 built, and is the oldest known coupe built in Stuttgart. *Steve Demosthenes*

and inquire about the rest of the Carrera, a 1956 sunroof model, originally aquamarine metallic.

"But what I had feared all these years finally happened: Paul died three weeks after I purchased the engine. He was sitting alone in his chair and was discovered by neighbors six days later. I contacted his brother, and I was finally able to acquire the Carrera body [in 2005]. This might be my last great barn find, but what a find it was!"

His final memorable Porsche-find tale starts while Demosthenes was traveling from Hood River, Oregon, back to the Florida Keys in his 1962 Notchback S90. Along the way, he hunted for old Porsches.

"While in Dallas, Texas, I was asking some local Porsche guys if they knew of any older Porsches for sale. I was told there was this weird, old professor in Denton, Texas, who had an ancient Porsche," he says. "The Pre-As [the very earliest] Porsches were not the 'hot topic' in those days. I drove up to see the car, and there it was, parked alongside the house. It was very, very rusty with years of moss, dirt, and leaves included. No one was home, so I took some photos and left a note."

Then, after Demosthenes returned to Key West, he got a call from the professor, who explained that he had bought the Porsche in Germany in the early 1970s. Years later, he shipped it to the United States, Alabama to be exact, and then the car made the move with

This photo of a coupe and a roadster was taken in the mid-1980s in a Gulfport, Mississippi, backyard. The owner wouldn't sell. Demosthenes believes that several hurricanes have most likely hit the area by now, and the cars—if still there—are likely totaled.
Steve Demosthenes

him to Texas. However, its time in Texas was pretty much spent sitting outside the garage, rusting.

Demosthenes first offer of $4,000 for the relic was happily accepted, and it wasn't until later that he discovered the uniqueness of his purchase. "The factory sent me the Kardex [or record sheet] for No. 5047, which confirmed it was built in August 1950 while Professor Ferdinand Porsche was still alive," Demosthenes says. "I tried to sell it in the States, but there were no takers. So I had a trip planned to Europe to visit as many Porsche guys as I could, from Sweden to Italy. While there, I met a collector in northern Italy who wanted the 356. He paid $15,000 for it."

At that point, the Porsche went into a five-year restoration, and a few years ago its current owner, a well-known Belgian collector, contacted Demosthenes about the car. "It turns out that it was the thirty-eighth 356 constructed in the Stuttgart factory, and reportedly the oldest 'known' coupe from Stuttgart," Demosthenes says.

Business is more difficult for this automotive archaeologist these days, as most of the great finds have been found. But like a good archeologist, he keeps digging. Over his nearly four decades of discovering and purchasing more than one hundred 356 Porsches, the market has changed. "It's not hard to sell 356s these days; it's just hard to find them. The 356 supply has dried up," he says. Today he and his wife operate from a 1923 building on Scenic Route 30 in Mosier, Oregon, overlooking the Columbia River Gorge. The 4,500-square-foot business, called Route 30 Classics, houses a vintage Porsche showroom, Porsche gift and memorabilia shop, and an adjoining gourmet ice cream and espresso shop.

"I am buying more early 911s now," he says regarding his current pursuit of Porsches. "As the age of the buyers get younger, it's the 1967 to 1973 Porsches they grew up dreaming about that they are buying. But that doesn't matter; it's all good."

This Coupe Ain't for Chickens

Billy Coates has two things going for him as a car hunter: he has a nose for sniffing out old cars and parts and an easygoing personality that convinces their owners into selling those nostalgic treasures off to him. As a result, he's one of the luckiest car guys around.

One of his luckiest barn-find stories comes from his search for just the right Austin-Healey 100—one he could convert to V-8 power. He ended up searching for more than a decade to find it. During that time, Coates most often followed up leads that led to nonexistent cars or rust buckets. However, one day he got a call from a buddy who said he thought he might know of a '56 Healey 100 for a decent price.

After driving an hour from his home near Charlotte, North Carolina, to Rock Hill, South Carolina, Coates found the car and the woman whose husband first owned it. The husband had died years back, and the car had been sitting there ever since.

Billy Coates checks out a nostalgic hot rodder's dream, a '32 Ford three-window coupe, for the first time. The former Toledo Autorama show car was parked in 1972 and saw daylight again when Coates purchased it twenty-five years later. *Billy Coates*

In the trailer and on its way to North Carolina. The coupe was extensively modified in the 1950s, using lead instead of Bondo in the top chop and molded rear fenders. *Billy Coates*

Even though it was a bit weathered, Coates knew at first sight that this was the Healey of his dreams and asked how much the woman would take for it.

"What would you do with it?" she asked.

He then explained his intentions to refurbish it so that it would resemble the Austin-Healey he had in his youth.

"Well, if you give it a good home, it's yours for free," she said.

Stunned, Coates couldn't pass up such a good deal, so an hour later, he loaded up the Healey on his trailer and headed back home to Charlotte.

But his luck didn't end there. From Crosleys, old Fords, sports cars, a Cushman scooter, and flathead Ford speed parts, Coates has gotten more than his share of free or cheap cars.

So it was just another day at the office when he received a call from his friend Larry Jensen, with whom he shared a passion for hot rods. Jensen told Coates that one of his wife's relatives up in Mansfield, Ohio, had a couple of old Ford coupes in the garage: a 1934 Ford three-window with a rumble seat and a 1932 Ford five-window.

"I called Larry's relative and asked about the '32, since Larry already said he wanted the '34," Coates says. "He told me the '32 had a real low top and an Oldsmobile 303-cubic-inch engine with a bad oil leak."

Like a photo from a 1950s issue of *Rod & Custom* or *Hop Up* magazine, the interior of the Deuce Coupe shows a period door-panel design, Auburn dashboard with "winged" Stewart-Warner gauges, and a 1939 Ford gearbox. *Billy Coates*

Of course, the hopeful hot rodders couldn't resist going to see the cars firsthand, so on November 17, 1997, they hooked up their trailers and headed up the highway with their sights set on Mansfield. "It was so cold. There were seven inches of fresh snow on the ground," Coates says. "We walked into the garage and I immediately went over to the '34, because Larry was nice enough to invite me along. It was actually a five-window coupe with only 44,000 miles on the odometer. The front bumper and taillights were changed to more modern units, probably from a '48 Ford, but the originals were on a shelf in the corner of the garage." The '34 also had been converted to hydraulic brakes.

As his friend was becoming acquainted with his new purchase, Coates walked over to look at the car of his interest, the hot rod.

Instead of being a five-window, the '32 was actually a three-window coupe. The car, a shade of burgundy, was considerably modified. The top was chopped about three inches and the doors had hand-painted lettering that spelled out "Autorama, Toledo, Ohio" on them. Apparently, this car had been used as a promotional vehicle for hot rod shows in the 1950s and 1960s.

The all-steel car also featured cycle front fenders, bobbed rear fenders, and a three-piece hood. The grille was leaded and peaked, had a three-inch dropped front axle, and eight Stewart-Warner winged gauges sitting in an Auburn dash panel. The odometer read only 3,900 miles.

Needless to say, Coates had to make the car his own, and he negotiated a bargain price right on the spot. "I paid him that day and loaded the car onto my trailer," he says. "I needed to use the winch because all four wheels were frozen. But once the winch started to drag it, each of the wheels loosened up."

When he unloaded the car at home, he started to investigate his new asset. All the bodywork on the car was done with lead, confirming Coates' suspicions that the car was rebuilt in the late 1950s. "The body was perfect, with no rust anywhere," says the proud owner. "The window regulators still worked perfectly and all the wood in the body was original and perfect."

The Olds engine had an Edmunds dual two-barrel carburetor manifold and a Mallory ignition. Coates didn't like the exhaust headers because they seemed to be homemade. The engine was backed up by a 1939 Ford gearbox and a stock 1932 rear axle.

"The guy I bought it from didn't build the coupe, but bought it in 1971 from Gary Mohr of Swanton, Ohio, for $550," Coates adds. It had been last registered in 1972.

Now Coates had the dilemma of what to do with his car. He likes to drive his hot rods—he's put more than 100,000 miles on his '36 Ford coupe—so he decided only to modernize the car for reliability without affecting its heritage.

So far he has installed a TCI dropped front axle with disc brakes, a Lincoln Zephyr three-speed gearbox mated to a 1940 Ford column shift, heat, air conditioning, and power seats. He's going to stick with a 1950s-style rolled-and-pleated interior, though, and he is keeping many modern improvements hidden from view.

But what about the engine? "I figure that engine's got 3,900 miles on it," he says. "I'm cleaning it up, but I'm not going to rebuild it." With Coates' luck, he'll get another 100,000 miles out of it. And what color will he paint it? Budweiser Red. A friend of his works for Dale Earnhardt Inc. and gave him some extra paint from NASCAR superstar Dale Earnhardt Jr.'s car. Wow, some guys really do have all the luck.

The Shelby Wrangler

These days Jerry Schacht spends his time tearing apart old U.S. Army Jeeps and restoring them, but it isn't his Jeeps—which can sell for $13,000 to $14,000—that serious car hunters find most interesting. It's his Mustangs.

Schacht, who makes his home in Decorah, Iowa, has dozens of Mustangs, and many of them are the kind that a wily character from Texas, named Carroll Shelby, put his magic touch on.

Schacht hails from a car-dealing family, so it's not a secret that his car passion comes naturally. His grandfather was a Ford dealer who sold Model Ts in the early 1900s to residents of Decorah and his father peddled Chryslers and Plymouths before World War II.

Aside from spending time running his own Ford dealership, Schacht also worked on his friend Ernie Tuff's Modified Sportsman race cars when Tuff raced at Daytona each February in the early 1960s. "I'd go to the Holman-Moody shops and buy parts, and we'd use Smokey Yunich's garage down in Daytona," he remembers.

The previous owner of this Mustang fastback must have replaced the left-front fender with one from a GT350 that had been given a graphic treatment. *Gail Rhoten*

A pretty blue-with-white-stripes GT350 sits in the dark awaiting someone to make an acceptable offer to purchase it from Jerry Schacht. *Gail Rhoten*

"I worked for the Ford dealership in town," he adds. "It was in 1965, and it was an awesome time. The dealership owner—who was my age—and I got along really good.

"When that dealership closed, I bought the body shop and would go to places like Chicago and Milwaukee and buy up salvage Mustangs to rebuild and sell."

"Once I met this guy and he had a real pretty white Shelby GT350 that he'd bought for his wife," Schacht says. "But she didn't like the car because it had too much power, and her husband realized that it would be ultimately cheaper to trade the car than to trade his wife." So Schacht offered him a deal. Schacht located a nice, albeit slow, Mustang fastback with a six-cylinder engine and automatic transmission, and he offered it to the man on an even trade. The car cost him $1,300.

The man took the offer, and Schacht was on his way to becoming a wheeler and dealer of Shelby Mustangs.

As the years passed, Schacht found that he could buy Shelby GT350s for as little as $400 and store them in a large building he constructed so they wouldn't deteriorate.

"Some cars had damaged frames, and some had no engines," he says. "I bought a nice '66 Shelby that ran in Minneapolis. I bought others in Des Moines and in Newton, Iowa. Some I bought from finance companies."

In the 1970s, Schacht had a vacant lot in town with more than 100 Mustangs parked on it. "If you talk to some old-timers in town, they all remember all the Mustangs I had collected on that lot," he says. At one time, he had so many Mustangs that he couldn't count all the carcasses.

Yet his special passion was not particularly Mustangs—of which he still has about eighty—it was Shelbys.

Eventually Schacht was forced to move his collection from his original location at the old Ford dealership into a forty-foot by eighty-foot storage shed, where he stored his five remaining Shelbys, door handle–to–door handle.

It didn't take long for news of Schacht's collection to reach enthusiasts, who would travel from far and wide to negotiate a purchase. "I bought this Shelby for four hundred dollars, and sold it for twenty thousand dollars, and it was pretty well stripped when I sold it," he says in amazement.

"But I've thrown some guys out of here because they aggravated me so much. They criticize me, saying these cars don't mean anything to me and that I should sell them. But I tell them that these Shelbys must mean more to me than anyone else because I still have them after forty years."

One of his favorite Shelby-related stories revolves around a 1967 GT500 rollover that he paid $400 for. It originally had two four-barrel carburetors, but had been pretty well stripped of its valuable pieces over the years. For at least fifteen years, the car sat on the ground, and it had begun to sink into the dirt. He offered it for sale for $1,000 to $1,200, but found no takers. "Then a Shelby collector heard about it and offered me six thousand dollars for it," he says. That buyer eventually fully restored the once-thought-hopeless fastback.

Recently Schacht opened up his shed after twenty years so the accompanying photos for this book could be taken. "It was like opening up a tomb," he says. "The cars in there, like No. 347, are pretty good cars. They don't need to be restored. I've never restored them, so when someone buys them, the new owners can say the cars had longtime ownership. I'll let someone from the younger generation enjoy them. I've already had my fun."

Dr. Zagato Reveals His Secret for Buying Not-for-Sale Cars

David Sydorick has never been a guy who spots magnificent cars hidden in garages or barns. Instead he is the one who ultimately secures these incredible machines that have been long locked away. His special gift is in changing the minds of owners with no desire to sell what he so dearly wishes to buy. Over the years, he has collected many great cars, from Ferraris and Maseratis to hot rods.

Along the way, he became infatuated with cars bearing the coachwork of the Italian firm Carrozzeria Zagato. Zagato built custom bodies for a limited number of automobile chassis, including Ferrari, Maserati, Alfa Romeo, and Aston Martin.

The following are the tales of three exceptional Zagato-bodied cars and the art, and occasional bit of luck, Sydorick employed to make them his own. They include a Maserati, an Aston Martin, and an Alfa Romeo.

Maserati Zagato A69CS No. 2121

With Zagato cars, "double-bubbles" are key, Sydorick says. "Double-bubble" refers to the cars' trademark twin-curve roof shape, but finding the cars with this unique design feature isn't easy. "Zagato made a run of nineteen or twenty cars, and maybe one or two of them were double-bubbles," he says. "Of the Maseratis, they made nineteen, and No. 2121, my car, is the only double-bubble car, which made it very special and obviously the one to collect."

Sydorick found out about the car in a chance visit from a fellow California resident, Sal DiNatale, who knew about David's flat-top Zagato Maserati.

"He had bought [the double-bubble] in 1959, when he owned a restoration shop in the [San Fernando] Valley," Sydorick says. "It was his daily driver. He also used this car to get parts and even as a loaner car to guys he was doing work for. This was in the 1960s. Everyone knew the car and it was always around."

Who knew what treasure was lurking behind this door in the rural Italian village of Sabico for all those years . .
David Sydorick

But at some point, Sal, a native Sicilian, decided to move back to his hometown, so he put the car, its parts, and the tools into a container and sent it to Italy. There it sat in a garage for more than a decade even as DiNatale gave up plans to move to Italy and stayed in California.

"Maserati books always said that this car was hidden somewhere in Sicily," Sydorick says. "But every Italian I ever knew said, 'No such thing. There are no Zagatos in Sicily. We would know if there were'."

That's why it was a shock for Sydorick to hear DiNatale say that not only did he know where No. 2121 was, but he was its owner.

"Of course, I tried to convince him to sell me the car on the spot," Sydorick says. "Over the next couple of years, my wife Ginny and I spent a lot of time with Sal. He'd come over for dinner and we became friends. It was at least two years before he finally said, 'Yes, I'll sell you the car.'

"Little did I know that the real adventure was just about to begin. . ."

A workman removes the last pieces of brick wall that provided "Sicilian security"–anti-theft protection for the rare Maserati. *David Sydorick*

By this point the friends had agreed on a price, but Sydorick had never seen the car. So he decided a trip to Italy was in order. He arrived on one cold February night, exhausted from his trek from California to Milan to Catana.

"Sal's daughter picked me up, and fortunately she speaks English," Sydorick says. "She took me up a hill to a little town called Sabico, Sal's birthplace. It was dark, it was scary, it was frightening. Then I saw this barn with all these vines hanging down, and I said to her, 'I recognize this barn.' She told me that the movie *The Godfather* was filmed there. . . . We then walked into the barn, and there was this single light bulb hanging from the ceiling. She reached up and gave it a turn; the light came on, and there was the car."

Its paint had been stripped, but its California license plate was still on, weathered and rusted. The tires were also flat, the plexiglass windows checked and faded, but the old registration papers were still inside.

189

Sitting in a brick barn that had once been used in a *Godfather* movie, the Zagato Maserati has such a beautiful shape that it is still evident even with the paint stripped off its voluptuous body. *David Sydorick*

Sal's daughter was flooded with emotion as she realized the car would soon be gone.

"This was the car her daddy took her to school in during her childhood in the San Fernando Valley," Sydorick says. "She had no interest in the enormous check I was about to hand her. The only thing she knew for sure was that her daddy's old car was going to go away. She didn't see it, she didn't use it, she didn't touch it, but the passion and the love for it was still there."

The next day, when Sydorick showed up with a truck to move the car, everyone in the town seemed to know the car was leaving its longtime home. "Everyone was there to see us unveil—unearth, if you will—this car," he says. "It was [behind] an awful steel roll-up door that obviously hadn't been up in many years, and between the steel roll-up door and the car was 'Sicilian security'—a three-foot-high brick wall. We had a tank of air to pump up the tires, and then

Sal DiNatale's grandchildren came out to the transporter to say goodbye to granddad's car before it headed back to California with new owner David Sydorick. Many years earlier, DiNatale had driven their mother to school each day in the car. *David Sydorick*

we broke down the wall. Sal's two grandsons and his son-in-law were there with a brick hammer knocking down the bricks. Then we put the car on the truck and brought it back to California."

Back in California, Sydorick held a party to celebrate his newest purchase, and, of course, Sal DiNatale, the longtime owner, was invited. "He just stood by the car all night, beaming and smiling," Sydorick says.

After the celebration, Sydorick went about the task of restoring the car—which turned out to be a lengthy process even though he had Zagato specialist Nino Epifani from Berkeley, California, handle it. "Zagatos routinely have lots of corrosion; mine, which was parked on a dirt floor, was particularly corroded. It's an all-aluminum body, but aluminum still corrodes," Sydorick says. "In all, it took about two-and-a-half to three years to restore."

When the restoration was complete, Sydorick took it to Pebble Beach, where the car received a first-in-class award in a field of tough competition.

A couple of years later, an all-star cast of judges—including comedian Jay Leno—discuss the double-bubble roof on Sydorick's car at the Pebble Beach Concours. *David Sydorick*

"It was beautiful, stunning, had a great story to it, and was a terrific example of Zagato coach building," Sydorick says, addressing the car's warm reception there. The car continues to draw raves from many admirers.

"But I remember in particular one gentleman at the Aston meet in Lime Rock," he says. "He was elegantly dressed, and he walked around and around the car. You could see his eyes were just all over the voluptuous bodywork. You could tell he just wanted to reach out and touch the rear quarter panels. Then he walked over to me—somehow he knew that I was the owner—looked me in the eye, and said, 'I bet you never say no to her'."

Aston Martin DB4GT/0187/L

When Sydorick looked to add an Aston Martin to his Zagato collection, he ended up pursuing a very rare model—a left-hand-drive Aston Martin DB4 GT. When he started his search, he knew that only six or seven of the left-hand-drive models had been produced and knew where two were—with owners Bob Stockman, past president of the Aston Martin Club, and Jerry Rosenstock of California.

But eventually, Sydorick found a third owner, a scientist from Fullerton, California, Nicholas Begovich. "He was a CalTech PhD and didn't really talk to anybody. He was in his eighties," Sydorick says. "And he had many cars in his garages; I'd say . . . a dozen in each of his two garages. He had purchased many of the cars he owned new from the factory, like a Porsche Speedster and a Porsche 904 racer. He'd buy a car at the factory, drive it around a little, then bring it home and take it apart."

While Begovich really didn't let people see his cars, Sydorick somehow had a friend who got him in. "He knew I was after the Aston because I was a Zagato collector," Sydorick says. "The car was sitting there in his garage, jacked up on jack stands with a car cover over it. On the first visit, I could tell by his body language that I was not to lift that cover. And I didn't, so on that first visit, I never did see the car.

"But my wife, Ginny, and I became friends with Nick and his wife Lee. We started to do things. He came to our house. I think in the end, Nick was kind of interviewing me and us. . . . These cars are his children. He had never sold a car."

Two and a half years later, Sydorick thought maybe his moment had come, when over dinner, Begovich asked if he really cared about his rare Aston Martin.

"'Nick, of course I do,'" Sydorick said.

"Well, good. Maybe we can talk about it next year," Begovich responded.

Another year passed, and yet the Aston was still sitting in Begovich's garage.

"Little did I know that Nick wanted to donate the car to Cal Tech, and that I would have to purchase the car from the school," Sydorick says. "He set up a trust and gave the trust to Cal Tech, and I turned the trust into cash."

Over all this time, Sydorick had seen the car a few more times and learned more about it, including that Begovich never really drove it or started it.

"He had also taken the back axle out of the car in 1971, and it was still out in 2001. I think he originally did some work on the gas tank or something. But the engine and everything else were still all together," Sydorick says. "The car is a 1961; they only made the Aston Zagato body for one year. It's not a double-bubble, but it's one of only six or seven left-hand-drive cars built. And it was in one man's hands for thirty-seven years."

When it finally came time for Sydorick to pick up the car, though, there was a problem. Begovich couldn't find its title, so the car sat in limbo.

"A month passes, another month passes, and I still didn't have the car. He told me, quote, 'The car's not ready for you to pick up yet.' Suddenly it dawns on me that Nick isn't ready for the car to go away. He knew it was going away, but he wasn't quite ready to see it go. . . . I figure he wasn't quite ready for that car cover to disappear. It had sat in that one spot for thirty-plus years, and it was the first time he had ever sold a car."

A few months later, Sydorick got the okay to bring over a truck and take the Aston Martin away. He celebrated the occasion with champagne along with representatives from Cal Tech.

Then came another tough challenge: what would Sydorick do with the car now?

"It was a very strange red-pinkish color, with bumpers on it that, in my opinion stole the beauty of the car's architecture," he says. "All Aston Zagatos also had three bumps on the hood, but mine had a scoop on it. I didn't like the scoop and I didn't like the bumps; I would have preferred the car without either. But it wasn't born that way. So I struggled with this responsibility issue about what I'm supposed to do with this thing. It became a psychological thing—was I supposed to please Nick, or was I supposed to please the Aston Martin Club? Or was I supposed to please the Pebble Beach judges or the Aston crowd in England? Or was I supposed to please myself?"

After awhile, he decided to consult Miles Collier—one of the great car collectors of all time, to see what he thought. His answer initially wasn't what Sydorick expected—"Let the car tell you," he said. Yet, then Sydorick knew exactly what to do.

"I had a second hood made without the bumps or scoop that I could interchange, and I designed the bumpers so they could easily be removed or installed," he says. "I also involved Nick in the restoration process, and he and I flew around the country and interviewed Aston specialists as close as California and as far away as Philadelphia [for the job]. Ultimately, I chose Steel Wings outside of Philadelphia. All they do, and all they've ever done, is Aston Martins, so they know the cars upside-down. They set out to produce the best Aston Martin of all time for me. I think they accomplished that."

Sydorick's proof of the car's excellence comes in the awards the Aston Martin has received since then, which include a first-in-class at Pebble Beach and firsts at Palos Verdes and then Newport. "Everywhere we've gone, the car has taken first," he says.

ALFA ROMEO—NO. 2211052 & NO. 2311214
Ever since its introduction in the 1930s, the Alfa Romeo 8C has been a well-loved car. But over the years, its status has risen so much that it has become the centerpiece for all great car collections. Collector Miles Collier owns one; so does Ralph Lauren. And of course, David Sydorick, wanted one, too, especially because the early models sported Zagato bodies.

He ended up finding two in the garage of Haig Ksayian, who lived in New Jersey. One had the Zagato body he really wanted; the other had a Castagna drop-head coupe body.

"Sometime in the 1950s, the owner took the engine out of the Castagna and put it in the Zagato, and put the Zagato's engine on the shelf. Then he put the Castagna in the barn," Sydorick says. "Everyone tried to buy these cars forever and ever. Everyone knew where they were stored; they knew their provenance and their history. Literally every major collector from around the world went to his doorstep to try and buy these cars."

They all came away empty handed—until a car broker called Sydorick, letting him know the owner was ready to sell. The phone call between Sydorick and the broker went something like this:

"He told me he had them for sale and asked, 'Do you want to buy them?'" Sydorick says. "He said that if I wasn't interested, he was sure that on the next phone call he made they'd be sold. So I said yes."

Within days Sydorick was on a plane, going to see the cars he had purchased sight unseen. He expected that the owner would have

This 1933 Alfa Romeo Castagna drophead coupe was owned by Haig Ksayian, who purchased it in 1942 for less than $1,500. *David Sydorick*

Sydorick believes this Alfa is the only unrestored 8C in the world, and it is original and complete, right down to the dual spare tires. He hopes that a class at Pebble Beach may one day feature unrestored cars. *David Sydorick*

a tough time giving them up, but he really didn't. "He didn't really seem to care that much," Sydorick says, noting the toughest part of the transaction ended up being getting the cars out of the garage.

"Because these cars didn't run, I couldn't call one of the standard classic car shippers, so I called a guy with a trailer to pick them up in New Jersey and bring them to California. It's a less romantic story than some of the others, but another instance where a guy has owned these cars for sixty years. Everyone knew about them, but nobody could ever buy them. People would come to his door with baskets full of money and Haig told them to go away. I went there with a check to buy the cars, but you're always nervous. You're flying, you're driving, you've got to wait for the trucks to arrive, but in the end, we got the cars," he says.

He bought both because he needed to make sure that he had all the parts so the Zagato engine could go back into the Zagato car, thus giving the 8Cs all matching numbers.

The engine was removed from the Castagna-bodied Alfa and used in a 1933 Zagato-bodied 8C when the latter's engine showed signs of low oil pressure. *David Sydorick*

"I hoped and prayed that all the parts in the bushel baskets were correct," he says. "For two weeks, I went through every single part on both engines, and believe it or not, they all matched. They had all the right numbers and were in good condition. I was fortunate that Haig had an appreciation for the cars and never let anyone pick parts out of the baskets."

CHAPTER SEVEN

Unconventional Discoveries

Marrying into a '32 Three-Window

When Jason Freitas was on his honeymoon in September 1999, the last thing he was thinking about was old cars. Freitas, who had helped his father work on old cars and tractors since he was a child, was honeymooning at Disneyland because he was a little bit low on cash for the Las Vegas trip he and his new wife, Heidi, had originally planned.

Little did he know he would soon hit the jackpot anyway.

While the young couple was enjoying their first week together as husband and wife, they decided to visit Heidi's grandparents, who lived only about a mile away from the theme park. "I already knew that Heidi's grandpa was a major gearhead in his early days and that he and his brother were big into restoring Austin-Healey 3000s," says

Freitas, who is a mechanic at a Ford dealership about 400 miles north of Anaheim. Actually, before he died recently, Grandpa's brother, Ron Yates, was nearing completion of a book on Austin-Healeys.

Besides Healeys, Grandpa had a hankering for a 1932 Ford three-window coupe. He had purchased a 1932 rolling chassis and a body several decades earlier and began to collect parts at swap meets with the intention of one day assembling a complete coupe. Yet before he had a chance to build the '32 from parts, he found a complete and original '32 three-window coupe in incredibly sound condition. In 1984, he sold the body and chassis to purchase his new find.

"Heidi's grandmother gave me the key to the shed and asked if I wanted to see Grandpa's stuff," Freitas says, recounting the visit. "She said that I was the only one she could trust to go into the

"Why don't you go out into the barn and see Grandpa's stuff," Grandma told Jason Freitas while he was on his honeymoon. What he found was the stuff of a hot rodder's dream: a stock '32 Ford three-window coupe. *Jason Freitas*

Freitas inherited Grandpa's coupe, which is incredibly solid and still has the original Ford dealership sticker on the dashboard, along with the factory tool kit. He drives it around the neighborhood and to his town's annual tractor show. *Jason Freitas*

garage and not damage anything. As I opened the door and turned on the lights, I saw two vehicles." It was no surprise to him to see a Healey 3000. Seeing the other, a '32 Ford, however, was quite a shock. Even though Freitas is a Chevy enthusiast, he knew how special this discovery was. Grandpa had purchased the car in the mid-1980s, but due to declining health in recent years, he never got around to the restoration. It was in the same condition as when he purchased it two decades earlier. "I must have looked at the car for an hour," he says. "I was fascinated with it."

Several months later, when the honeymoon was over and the Ford was just a pleasant memory, Freitas received a phone call from Grandma. She and Grandpa had discussed giving the Ford coupe a good home, and they had decided that Freitas could provide that home. "I was written into their will. I would receive the coupe when Grandpa passed on," he says. "I was completely flattered."

Not too long later, Freitas received another phone call from Grandma. She and Grandpa had discussed the car again, this time deciding that he could pick up the car anytime he liked.

"I had a three-day weekend coming up and told her I'd be down to pick it up," Freitas says. "I borrowed a pickup truck and a trailer and was there a month later. My goal was to bring it home that Sunday and have it running for the tractor show in Galt [California] the following weekend. I'd go there every year with my dad."

When the rare three-window coupe—every hot rodder's dream— was pushed out of the garage and onto the waiting trailer, it was the first time the car had seen daylight in many years. After it was loaded and tied down, Freitas said thank you and goodbye to Grandpa and Grandma and headed on down the road for the trip home.

When he got there, he and his father started to inspect the coupe from bumper to bumper. It was evident that he had inherited quite a special car. "My father is sixty-two years old, and he said even when he was in high school, they were pretty rare," Freitas says.

The car has a number of rare features: the original Murray Body Company badge is still mounted on the lower cowl; the rearview mirror has an optional clock that still works; the right side of the dashboard has a sticker from the Los Angeles Ford dealer that sold the car new; and the trunk has a spare tire lock, jack, tools, a light bulb kit, and a combination wheel wrench and engine crank. Plus Freitas kept all the spare 1932 Ford parts that Grandpa had purchased for his earlier coupe project.

"When I picked up the car, Grandma told me to look through the bookshelves, and to take any book that had to do with old Fords," he says.

Within four days of his 400-mile tow, Freitas and his father had the Ford running. "She fired right up and ran just fine," he says. "I pull the choke and it starts every time.

"My dad lives near our home but out in the country, so it's no problem driving it around his town on Sunday afternoons. Plus, I drive it each year to the tractor show. That's when all the old-timers come up and ask, 'Where did you get something like that?' and I say, 'I married the right woman.' Then they ask, 'How much did you pay?' and I say, 'Nothing.' Then they ask, 'How'd you do that?' and I say, 'It's called inheritance'."

Freitas doesn't ever plan to restore his inheritance. The body is very sound, with almost no rust. The interior was redone in an incorrect tuck-and-roll pattern, probably in the 1950s, but that will stay as well.

When Freitas' first daughter, Emma, was born, Grandma and Grandpa drove up for the baby shower. "So I had the car ready and I had the honor of giving him a ride in his old '32 Ford. He was quite tickled."

These days, the Freitas household has two children running around, and money isn't flowing as much as it once did. But the coupe sits quietly in Jason's father's barn, just a few miles away. He checks it out once in a while and he still drives it on occasion, but mostly he's just pleased that he was chosen to be the car's caretaker.

"I've had lots of opportunity to sell it, but I'm only twenty-nine years old, so I still have lots of time to enjoy it," he says. "I don't plan to part with it any time soon."

Tax Benefits

You find cars where they are—sometimes they're found in barns, sometimes in warehouses, or even in fields or garages. And sometimes they appear at Internal Revenue Service auctions, which is where Gary Moore bought a once-famous, and soon-to-be-famous-again, '39 Ford woody wagon.

Moore and his wife, Elisa, had always craved a life near the ocean, so in the early 1990s, they packed up their possessions and moved from Kansas City, Missouri, to Melbourne, Florida. Shortly after arriving on the East Coast, the lifelong car enthusiast was scanning the *Florida Today* newspaper and a classified IRS ad caught his attention. It listed an old woody wagon for sale. "I called the local IRS office and learned that it was an orange 1939 Ford woody, actually one that I had spotted on a beach road on earlier visits to the area," Moore says. "So I submitted a sealed bid for just a little bit more than I thought everyone else's bid would be, and enclosed a twenty percent deposit in the form of a cashier's check."

Upon inspection, Moore saw that the car needed lots of work. It had a tired 283-cubic-inch Chevy with a Powerglide transmission and

The way the wagon looked before Gary Moore purchased it at an IRS auction. Note the rare, original surf decals on the back windows that the IRS had scraped off before Moore picked up his new car. *Gary Moore*

Moore's '39 woody has been featured in two movies. Here, actors Don Knotts (passenger) and Tim Conway (driver) appear in the car during shooting of *The Detectives*.
Gary Moore

it rested on a dropped front axle with worn-out kingpins. It was rough, but it was a woody, and Moore was hoping not too many people would respond. He did not attend the auction several weeks later, figuring he would be outbid anyway. Then when a local woody enthusiast, Bill Lutter, called him from the U.S. Government complex and informed Moore that his bid was the highest by $51. Moore was ecstatic now that he owned the car of his dreams. But Lutter also wanted to own the woody, and he wanted to buy it right on the spot. "To save a lot of dickering and getting his hopes up, I told him the car would cost $15,000, or roughly twice my winning bid," Moore says. "He almost hung up on me, but later we became good friends and still laugh about it today."

Moore picked up the car a few days later from the IRS impound yard and was shocked to discover that the IRS had given it to a local automotive detail shop to clean up. Unfortunately, the cleanup included taking a razor blade to the 1960s surf decals that were displayed on the side windows, some of which were irreplaceable.

On his way home, Moore drove the car cautiously. Because of its sloppy front suspension, it changed lanes at will. The brakes also barely functioned and the tailpipe put out a smoke screen plume.

Over the next few weeks, he continued to drive the car in its as-found condition, and he also began to learn much of the woody's history from some of the locals. He discovered that the woody had been a true California surf wagon when it was purchased in the 1970s and then moved east. And after some further detective work,

Moore found the first East Coast owner and discovered that the car had been rented for the filming of the 1978 movie *The Detectives*, starring Don Knotts and Tim Conway. At the time, the car was painted dark brown and was chosen because it had an air conditioning system. The movie was actually shot around the Biltmore Estate in Asheville, North Carolina.

The woody was later purchased by the owner of Sundeck Swimwear and relocated to Melbourne, Florida. It was used as a prop in numerous catalogs and surfing magazines, and after it received a bright orange paint job, it was used in Ron Jon's Surf Shop ads for several years.

When Moore became its new owner, the woody was pretty much worn out. He realized that he would need to modernize the car to make it drivable. He decided to have the car torn down to its chassis and modified with a Mustang II independent front suspension, as well as power steering and power brakes. A new Chevy 350 crate engine was installed, backed up by a 350 turbo transmission and Chevy Nova rear end. Additionally new air conditioning, a CD player, and cruise control were added. Then Erik Johnson of Treehouse Woods in Cocoa Beach replaced the deteriorated wood and refitted the doors and tailgate. Finally, the car was refinished in

Hard to believe it's the same car, Moore's woody takes on a completely different look with a new coat of teal paint and alloy wheels. Moore also installed a 350 Chevy engine, an automatic transmission, and air conditioning in it. *Gary Moore*

1995 Ford Mustang teal basecoat/clearcoat paint, and polished American Racing mags were installed.

Not one to waste time, Moore drove the car to Indianapolis for the Goodguys hot rod show just two days after it was completed. From there he continued west to Springfield, Missouri, for the 1993 *Rod & Custom* Americruise. Eventually the car was featured in *Rod & Custom* magazine and appeared on the cover of *Streetscene*.

Due in part to the woody's spectacular colors, and in part to its notoriety, a film production company contacted Moore about using the car in a surf movie called *The Last Perfect Wave*. The car was used for about two weeks, but seldom driven. Instead the car was dragged on an open trailer as driver and passengers pretended to drive the woody. Lights, cameras, and batteries were mounted on the front fenders and rear tailgate, but surprisingly no damage occurred during the course of filming.

While the car was being filmed, it caught the attention of an airline pilot from Hawaii, and he tracked Moore down to make an offer to buy it. A deal was struck, and the pilot drove the car across the United States with his nephew. When it arrived in California, it was loaded onto a plane and sent to Hawaii.

Moore doesn't have regrets about selling the classic car because shortly afterwards he bought another woody—this one a 1950 Ford. He's also bought several more barn finds since then and continues to scan the IRS auction ads. Because the cars are where you find them, you know.

Here the car is rigged for a simulated driving sequence in its second movie, *The Last Perfect Wave*. Moore has since sold the car to an airline pilot in Hawaii. *Gary Moore*

A Shotgun, a Hired Dick Tracy, and the California Kid

"**G**et off my property," the old woman said as she raised the shotgun to her shoulder. But getting killed was not part of Jim Locke's plan. He and a friend had driven out to the country to see a car, one they'd heard rumors about in the mid-1980s, but early on their treasure hunt appeared doomed.

The quest had begun several months earlier—after Locke and his son Jamie had a drag racing club event and hit the jackpot (the barn hunter's jackpot, that is). "This guy told us about this old red hot rod coupe he saw around town only once and never again," says

After years of hearing rumors, Jim Locke was finally able to see the mysterious '34 Ford coupe thanks to help from a private investigator. Here is what he found in the Oklahoma chicken shack in 1989. *Jamie Locke*

Jamie, now 32. "My dad became interested, since he's lived his whole life in this town, so he asked a friend of his who is a private investigator to see if he could locate the car."

A couple of weeks later, Jim Locke's detective friend called and said he found the car. "What car?" Locke asked, forgetting about the earlier conversation. "I know where the coupe is," his friend reiterated.

Suddenly, it clicked. The coupe that had been seen only once—and that had been the talk of car people all over Tahlequah, Oklahoma, since—had been discovered.

"But the person who has it is a widow, and she's not very inviting," the detective warned Locke.

The next morning the two drove out to the country, to an old, decrepit house. The weeds in the driveway were overgrown and it was obvious that whoever lived here didn't get out much.

As they approached the house, the woman—Mrs. Abadjian—came out the door toting a shotgun. "Get off my property," she said, and Locke and his friend quickly retreated. But over the next few months, they went back several times, and they got closer to the house each time. Then they thought they were ready to have a conversation with Mrs. Abadjian. They walked up on the porch, had some small talk, and then uttered the word "car." "Get off my property," she said again. Obviously, Mrs. Abadjian knew what they were after, and she didn't want any part of it.

Locke had all but given up on pursuing whatever hot rod coupe was sitting in Mrs. Abadjian's garage when he decided to give it one more try several months later. He walked up to the porch, expecting a shotgun reception, and a man walked out of the front door. "Who's this?" Locke thought. It was Mrs. Abadjian's brother, who had apparently just lost his wife. He had come to Oklahoma to collect his sister and move with her to Baja, California, to live out their years together.

Locke's visit turned out to be perfect timing.

"So you're here to talk about the car," the brother said, and then he led Locke into an old chicken shack in the backyard. Still not knowing what kind of car it was, Locke assisted in peeling back the heavy, oily cloth that covered the car in its dusty confines.

When they were finally done unwrapping, there it stood: the prettiest 1934 Ford three-window coupe you ever did see. It was faded red with a Buick "nailhead" V-8 engine, six Stromberg carburetors, a four-speed Muncie gearbox, and Stewart-Warner gauges. But what really attracted Locke to the car was the perfect body. He had to own it.

They negotiated a price and Locke ran to the bank in town to get a cashier's check drawn. But Mrs. Abadjian was leery of Locke, and thought that he might have, in fact, forged the check himself. So Locke ran back to town and withdrew enough cash to buy the coupe. Only when he presented Mrs. Abadjian and her brother with a sack full of cash did they let him load the car onto the trailer.

Once Locke handed over the cash, Mrs. Abadjian began to open up about his new purchase's history. Turns out that her husband, Abby Abadjian, was a hot rodder of some repute in California. "My husband worked for Pete & Jake's and was their right-hand man in the shop," she said. Apparently, Abby had reworked the '34 two or three separate times between his stays in prison.

"When some movie producers went to Pete & Jake's about a car for the movie *The California Kid*, they saw my husband's car, and said they wanted that for the movie," she said. But Abby was in prison, so either Pete or Jake said that wasn't possible and they offered to build a car just like Abadjian's for the movie.

People who knew Abby Abadjian—coworkers, hot rodders, even Pete Chapouris and Jim Jacobs—didn't give Jim Locke many answers about the guy. "He was a talented tile setter," is all they say.

So to find out more about the car's history, Jamie Locke started to buy old collections of hot rod magazines. "I have pictures of it from the March 1978 *Street Rodder* magazine, in a story about the last race at Irwindale Speedway," he says.

Eventually, Jamie moved to Dallas, Texas, for work and his dad used the old coupe less and less.

When it was dragged out of the shack, the coupe's unusual Buick engine was exposed. The car's original builder, Abby Abadjian, fabricated the unique injector stacks onto the coupe's six carburetors. *Jamie Locke*

When Jamie began to hang around at a street rod shop outside of Dallas, Sachse Rod Shop, he told the guys there all about the car that was back home, in his dad's garage. "But after hearing my story for seven years, I think they began to wonder if my story was real or not," Jamie says.

They found out after Jamie and his wife bought a house and Jamie's dad traded him the coupe for a new Harley.

"Dad had begun to be somewhat disenchanted with the car," Jamie says. "It was an insurance payment he didn't need, and whenever he wanted to take it for a drive, it took half a day just to get it started. So we wrote out an agreement on a paper napkin where I promised I wouldn't butcher the car up, and now it's mine for life."

Jamie eventually trailered the car home and drove it unannounced into the parking lot at the Sachse Rod Shop. "The whole place emptied out to look at the car, the employees and the customers," he says. "They all went bonkers; it was the hit of the afternoon.

"'Look at this, and look at that' is all I heard. George Packard, the general manager of the shop, said to me, 'This is more than I ever thought you had.'"

A master craftsman, Abadjian fabricated a custom dash and steering column that impressed even street rodders like Jim Jacobs. *Jamie Locke*

Turns out that Packard was going to the Street Rod Nationals in Louisville the following week, and he was planning to have dinner with Jim Jacobs. He hoped that at the dinner he could find out more about Jamie's car.

"When he came back from the nationals, he said he had learned more about my car than he thought he could learn," Jamie says. "Jim remembered the car like it was yesterday—the killer dash, the aluminum steering column, the ladder-bar rear end. But I wanted to know about the man, Abby.

"What Jim told [Packard] was that if you look at a crowd of 1,000 people, you can spot a guy in that crowd you wouldn't mess with. Abby was that guy. He was the nicest, most lovable guy in the world if he liked you. If he didn't like you, you had trouble."

People were eager to talk about the '34, but still hesitant to discuss Abadjian even many years after his death.

What Jamie was able to find out about Abadjian was that he was an incredible craftsman. While he was employed at Pete & Jake's, he would allow others to help him fabricate parts, like the dash that

When son Jamie Locke took ownership of the coupe, he trailered it to Dallas, where it became the hit of the local hot rod scene. He has no intention of restoring the car; instead he hopes to preserve the work of a master craftsman. *Jamie Locke*

Jacobs helped fabricate or the steering column that Chapouris helped build. But only Abadjian himself could install it on his coupe.

To look at Abadjian's work today, it's as if this mysterious master craftsman's project was put into a time capsule. It is so well engineered, sometimes to the point of frustration. "One of the rear wheels was bent, so I brought it to a wheel repair shop to have straightened, and they said, 'We have no idea what kind of wheel this is,'" Jamie says. "Apparently the outer rims were from a different car than the inner rims, which were attached by a steel band to widen the wheels. And the hub was from a different car as well."

Thankfully, Jamie Locke is content with his coupe the way it is. He doesn't plan to change a thing about it. "I love the car for what it is," he says. "I wouldn't restore this car even if I could afford to. It's good enough to drive to local car shows and to go to the hamburger stand."

By leaving this barn find untouched, Jamie is also paying tribute to the strange, mysterious craftsman whom people are still hesitant to discuss, Abby Abadjian.

Surfin' Safari

By Kris Palmer

David Luchsinger is not a hunter, but he's glad one of his coworkers is. While hunting duck and pheasant on a northern California ranch, the coworker got caught in a downpour and ran for shelter in an old barn on the property. As he waited for the rain to back off, he looked around inside the barn and saw something in the corner under a tarp—an old car's unmistakable lines.

When he got back from the hunting trip, he told David about the find as everyone around the Pacific Bell knows David as the car guy. He was intrigued. His colleague then said he was going back to the ranch the next weekend, so David sent his Polaroid camera with him and asked him to snap a few pictures of the car.

He brought the camera and the photos back the following Monday. The first shot got David's blood flowing—it showed a 1940 Ford standard grille. Luchsinger's a hot rod guy, and he was looking for a 1940 to be his next rod. He wanted a closed car that he could use in cooler weather. He'd also seen a '40 that Roy Brizio did for Eric Clapton. "I'd like to build one like that," he thought.

The fact that his colleague had stumbled upon the exact car David was looking for seemed too good to be true, though from the next shot, he could see the front clip—undamaged. The third photo showed the body, and David's hopes were dashed. The car hidden in the ranch barn was a woody! It was not, in David's mind, the stuff of a great hot rod.

Luchsinger spent the next couple of days talking and joking about the car with his hot rod buddies. They laughed at how ugly the woody was. The car was in his head, though. It seemed like a part of his mind was looking for a way to like this hidden treasure. Then Luchsinger remembered something hot rod guru Mickey Lauria had said in an interview: that he thought the next big fad was going to be woodies. David had another look at the pictures. He asked his hunter-colleague

As it was dragged out of a northern California barn, new owner David Luchsinger's $3,000 purchase appealed to several other motorists, who offered to buy it for more than three times that amount. *David Luchsinger*

what the rancher wanted for it. The answer was $3,000—enough for the rancher to pay off a used pickup he'd bought.

David picked up the phone and called the seller. Then he visited a bank, hooked up his car trailer, and told work his buddy they were calling in sick. The old car bug had gotten through his body's defenses.

It was Friday, early, and a four-hour drive to the ranch. They got some coffee and hit the road. As they neared their destination, the road started to disappear. First the pavement went, then most of the road width. Luchsinger and his colleague were pulling a twenty-one-foot trailer down two rutted tire tracks. David started looking for a place to turn around, but the barn appeared first.

The rancher had been waiting for "the boys from the city." He invited them in for some homemade wine—even though it was ten o'clock in the morning. They talked as they drank.

The rancher was the original owner of the car, which he bought new in San Francisco. He moved it to the ranch in the early 1960s, where he used it to shuttle his large family around the property. It hadn't been off the ranch since. He asked if they wanted to take it for a ride. David nearly spit wine on his friend as he blurted, "It runs?!" The rancher answered, "You bet."

Out at the car, Luchsinger saw that the woody wore original plates, with current registration. They pushed it from the barn, installed a fresh battery, and hit the starter. After a few cranks, the old flathead coughed to life. It wasn't firing on all eight cylinders, but it was running. With a short drive around the ranch, David knew his $3,000 was not coming home.

The drive back was more eventful than the early run north. Out on the highway, a car pulled up behind them, honking its horn and flashing its lights. Was there something wrong with the car? Was something dragging? David pulled into a rest stop and the other driver ran over, extremely excited about the car. He had heard there was an old woody in the area and had searched for it for years, without luck. This had to be the one. He offered Luchsinger $5,000 on the spot. David had to think—he could nearly double his money. But he said no.

Later, while stopped for gas, a similar incident occurred. Another car stopped and its two occupants ran over to the trailer. They were headed to an old car auction in San Francisco, where they hoped to buy a woody. They thought David was bringing the car there to sell. They also offered $5,000. They even offered to buy the trailer, or pay David to deliver the car. David told them he'd already turned down that amount, and they doubled it. He sent the two men on to San Francisco, empty-handed.

By now Luchsinger and his colleague knew they were onto something good. Back at his house, they couldn't resist taking the car for

Halfway through the woody's two-year rebuild. Luchsinger and his buddy test-fit a new wood body to the '40 chassis.
David Luchsinger

another spin. His friend grabbed his boom box and a Beach Boys CD, and they took the old car cruising to the strains of "Surfin' Safari."

David's plan was still to turn this vehicle into a hot rod—but he changed his vision when he began to call around about parts. When he told a man he'd called from an ad in *Hemmings* that he had a 1940 standard woody, the man was impressed to the point of doubt. He asked Luchsinger if he would mind telling him the VIN number. David told him and the man responded, "You've got a really rare car there. Not many around." David has since learned that 8,730 of the 1940 woodies were DeLuxe models. Only 4,469 were built as standards.

His new plan soon changed to making the woody a resto rod, basically keeping his barn find stock, with a modified flathead, but restored to original condition. If fate had been leading him toward a wood-bodied car, it had set good groundwork. David's best friend was a pattern-maker with a full wood shop. David called him about the car and he said, "Let's get started." He would do the body, while Luchsinger did all the metal and mechanical work. They sourced some hard rock maple, similar to the wood used to build the car.

As time passed, David became so passionate about his Ford woody that he and his friend worked on it virtually every day for the next two years. David would work eight hours at his regular job, come home, and then put another eight into the car.

As the two-year anniversary of working on the car approached, David nearly had it finished. But Luchsinger decided it needed one final touch one night. He worked on it the rest of the night wiping everything down, washing and waxing it until it shined like a new car. Then he pushed it out into the driveway where all the neighbors could see it.

When morning came, they started coming over. All of them wanted to know if this was—if it could possibly be—the same tired, old car he'd brought home from the barn two years earlier.

A lot had changed with the car. David sold his other hot rods and joined Santa Cruz Woodies, the largest club chapter in the country. But some things hadn't—David had kept looking for old projects and parts over the years. In fact, that's how he found the woody's second engine. (Don't worry, David has the original powerplant, restored as new.)

Every day while Luchsinger worked on the chassis, an elderly couple would walk past. One day they stopped by David's driveway and he heard the woman say to her husband, "Go ask him." They had seen David out there working on old cars and were wondering if he might be interested in some parts. Their son had collected an assortment years ago, but now they were selling the property and their realtor told them they needed to clear it all out. Ever the optimist, Luchsinger said sure, he'd come have a look.

When he got there, he could see that it was old stuff. Some of it was covered up. But when he looked beneath some canvas, his jaw dropped. Among the parts was a flathead V-8, built up with all the vintage race goodies—aluminum manifold, special heads, and Stromberg carburetors. David told the couple, yes, he could help them out with removing this stuff. That engine is now a backup, built up exactly the way a California hot rodder would have done it in the 1950s and 1960s.

Luchsinger still has the woody and its future is specified in his will. His wife is a fan too and they're looking for one to build up for her. He has many friends into these cars now and loves the club members. He finds that "the people who own woodies are really unique—really great people." You might have a rare, concours woody worth $100,000 at a club event, and someone else will drive in with one completely rotted out and held together with duct tape. People are just as interested in the tattered car and its story as the spotless show-condition one.

He's become an expert himself at finding woodies ready for restoration. One turned up just a few miles from his house, on a plot of land he'd driven by every day for thirty-five years. It belonged to a small corporation and its owner had tucked a woody away in one of the buildings. One day, there it was, a 1939 Ford woody pushed out into the yard. Luchsinger hit the brakes, leapt from his car, and might have cleared the fence in one leap if he'd tried.

He found the owner and asked him to sell the car. The owner refused. David stayed in touch and one day asked the owner to come to his house and see his car. The sight of David's pride and joy, restored the way Ford built it more than a half-century before, affected the owner. Luchsinger said it wasn't fair to leave the '39 woody sitting until it deteriorated to the point where no one could bring it back. Hearing of the passion that people have for these cars, and seeing the great work David did on his, made the man relent. He said he would sell.

David called a friend who had been searching for one and told him he had found a 1939 woody for him right by his house. It was here waiting for. . . . There was a pause and David suddenly found himself talking to the friend's wife. He asked where his buddy was. His wife said, "He's out in the garage hooking up his trailer."

That car is being restored now, another woody that will know a new life, new miles, new pride, and friendships—all because a nosy hunter took refuge from the rain in an old barn in northern California.

Hard to believe it's the same car: Luchsinger's 1940 Ford woody is a show stopper. The car retains the original drivetrain, but the flathead engine has been mildly modified. *David Luchsinger*

From Behind the Iron Curtain

Along with its greater horrors, World War II destroyed objects of beauty beyond counting. Many rare and fascinating cars were lost to the ravages of warfare; others were confiscated and used to transport officers and most of those disappeared too. A few, like the Paris-Salon Delahaye model 135M profiled here, survived into the twenty-first century through a combination of careful planning and luck.

The car was built for a Bohemian businessman named Adamek in 1937. He had seen a similar car at the Paris Automobile Show the previous year. That car, with coachwork by Figoni et Falaschi of Paris' Boulougne-sur-Seine area, sold to Indian Prince Aly Khan for the incredible price of $27,000 U.S. dollars. Mr. Adamek wanted a car like it with the same company's coachwork.

He placed his order through the Vienna Delahaye agent, Hoffman and Hupport, for a 1937 model. The Delahaye company obliged by

This rare Delahaye was purchased new by an Austrian businessman in 1937, then put into hiding during World War II, when most other prestigious marques were converted to military use. *Jacques Harguindeguy*

manufacturing Competition Chassis No. 48666 and shipping it off to Figoni et Falaschi. The coachbuilder installed body No. 676, a short wheelbase "Competition Court," or "Roadster Grand Sport," model. The car was painted an elegant "gris lumière et rouge foncé"—a very light gray with deep red trim.

When the war started, Adamek had the foresight to hide the car, which protected it from confiscation. After the war, the Delahaye No. 48666 was resurrected and driven throughout northern Bohemia through the 1950s and 1960s. Records suggest that it was once raced on an amateur level during its life in Czechoslovakia.

In 1969, the fabulous Delahaye, like so many cars before it and after, found its way into a barn. The man who bought it intended to restore it, but he never found the time. For the next three decades, the Delahaye sat disassembled in a barn just outside Prague, its Figoni et Falaschi coachwork and other parts hanging from the walls.

Its owner knew the car's value and had some idea on whom to get word to when he decided to sell. That word reached Jacques Harguindeguy through a Delahaye parts seller he liked to spend time with at Retromobile, Paris' week-long parts swap meet.

Shortly after the 1997 Retromobile, that friend called Harguindeguy with a unique opportunity: a sixty-year-old Delahaye, disassembled and concealed for half its life in a Prague barn, was up for sale. "When he described the car to me, I told him that I would give my balls for a car like that," Harguindeguy says. "He said that nobody else knew about this car, but I only had three days to give him my decision."

That was Friday, so Harguindeguy asked for, and thankfully received, two extra days, so he could investigate the car among French collectors. "On Monday I got hold of the archivist for the Delahaye club in France," he says. "He actually knew about the car, but said the old gentleman who owned it wanted $250,000 for it, which, in his mind, was way too much money. I was very nervous, because there are lots of fake ones around. He told me that even though it was in poor condition and disassembled, it was authentic."

Having made it through the war, the Delahaye, now in Czechoslovakia, was raced for a while, then disassembled for a restoration that was never completed. Here, the car is bolted together for shipment to the United States in 1997. *Jacques Harguindeguy*

Harguindeguy had another friend, Christoph Grohe of Switzerland, travel to Prague to see the car in person. Before he arrived in Prague, Grohe was suspicious that the car might be a replica. But upon seeing the car, and discovering that the Figoni et Falaschi body was indeed genuine, he knew that he was in the presence of a very special car. Even though it was disassembled, the car showed traces of its original pearl gray paint, dark red accents, and red leather interior. The car seemed to be complete, but was missing its cosmetic chrome trim and a radiator.

"I said 'Thank you very much,' and bought the car," Harguindeguy says. "I was amazed that even though the car was apart and had been neglected for decades, the original engine with the correct No. 37 stamping was still with the car. This was rare."

Harguindeguy had struck a deal, but the purchase was only a step in getting the car. Next came the tricky business of removing it from the Czech Republic. "The car was totally in pieces, so we had to pay lots of under-the-table money to government officials to get it out of the country," he says. "When it arrived in Switzerland, I had the car loosely assembled so it would fit into a shipping container."

The car was then shipped to Harguindeguy's California home in 1998. Restoration began in March 1999, and it took approximately two years to complete. He worked closely with Brian Hoyt of Perfect Reflections in Haywood, California, whose shop restored the car as Harguindeguy conducted research and sourced parts. "The engine block was in very bad shape," he says. "It had frozen and was cracked, but we saved it. I bought three Delahayes to restore this one."

One of the toughest jobs was recasting the elegant brightwork that runs around the headlights and taillights and the trim on the fenders. Using only blurry pre-war photos of his car and other Figoni et Falaschi models of the era, Harguindeguy and his restorers exquisitely reproduced the trim in solid brass before sending it to the platers.

Harguindeguy received the car from the restoration shop in July 2000, when he brought it to the upholstery shop to have its unique bench front-seat interior trimmed. One month later, he trailered the Delahaye to Pebble Beach for the annual Concours d'Elegance. In contrast to most of the other owners of classic cars, though, he didn't show the car to anyone during the days leading up to the Sunday classic. "I kept the car hidden in my trailer prior to the show," he says, not wanting the politics of car judging to "predetermine" his car before the show.

By coincidence, Claude Figoni, son of the co-founder of the famous Figoni et Falaschi coach-building team, was invited in 2000 to Pebble Beach as grand marshal. "I only showed Claude the car in the trailer on Saturday, and a little tear came to his eye," Harguindeguy says. "He said it looked like it left our shop yesterday."

Early on Sunday morning of the fiftieth Pebble Beach event, Harguindeguy opened the trailer, backed his car out, and drove it toward the legions of car fans and the judges. The crowd was floored

During restoration in California, the Delahaye went through numerous test fittings to ensure the exotic bodywork would measure up to the highest concours standards. *Jacques Harguindeguy*

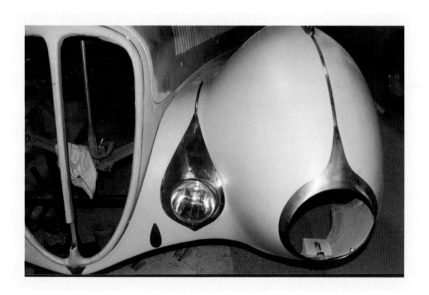

Most of the beautiful trim that surrounded the headlights and driving lights had been lost during its long disassembly in Czechoslovakia, so Jacques Harguindeguy had to fabricate new pieces from solid brass. *Jacques Harguindeguy*

All the years of hard work and searching the globe for parts pays off: Harguindeguy and his daughter, Debbie Wall, drive across the reviewing stand when the Delahaye was chosen Best of Show at the 2000 Pebble Beach Concours. *Jacques Harguindeguy*

by the car's beauty, its elegant lines, and beautiful details. Clearly the car was a show favorite, but Harguindeguy wouldn't know which car won the coveted Best of Show until all the award winners were driven across the judging stand. As he and his daughter, Debbie Wall, drove the Delahaye across the stand, in front of the thousands of spectators, a confetti cannon exploded and rained colored ribbons on his car. Harguindeguy had won the most prestigious award in the world of car collectors.

The Delahaye that survived the war, some amateur racing, and a long stint scattered about a Czech barn was finally recognized as the best in the world. Once more it boasted the beauty and artistry with which it entered the world in an earlier century. But additional showing for the car was of no interest to Harguindeguy. "It's already won the biggest award in the world," he says. "What could be better than that?"

Flea Market Photos Lead to Unusual, One-Off Truck Find

Jim Degnan already had a unique car transporter, a converted Olds Tornado airport limo, when he saw another one and decided he had to have it. Degnan didn't see the actual hauler, but a picture of it, while flipping through a box of discarded magazine photos at a flea market. It was a Cheetah transporter, custom made by Norm Holtkamp in the early 1960s, and modeled after a high-speed Mercedes-Benz hauler.

There was no guarantee that the car still existed, yet Degnan set out to find it. He guessed that if it was still around, it would be in Southern California, so he started to make some calls.

He first asked his sports car and hot rod buddies to see if they knew the whereabouts of this vehicle. "Then I spoke to Tom Medley, who was the cartoonist for *Hot Rod Magazine*'s Stroker McGurk. Medley knew that Norm Holtkamp was the original builder and

West Coast racer Norm Holtkamp became so inspired by the Mercedes-Benz race car hauler of the 1950s that he decided to build an American version to haul his own racers to the track. Here Holtkamp (driving the truck), driver Jack McAfee (in the race car), and crew member Harry Jones load up McAfee's Willment racer onto the unique hauler. *Jim Degnan Collection*

226

The inspiration for Holtkamp's transporter came from a photo he had seen of the Mercedes race transporter in *Road & Track* magazine. The Mercedes used a 300SL engine and transported the W196 or SLR race cars to tracks around Europe in excess of 100 miles per hour. Holtkamp had hoped his transporter would exceed 110 miles per hour. *James Degnan Collection*

that he still lived in Califorina. So I found his phone number and called him."

That's when Degnan got the whole story.

Norm Holtkamp, a former midget racer from northern California, began thinking about building a high-speed race hauler after seeing a Mercedes hauler profiled in a 1950s edition of *Road & Track* magazine. He was intrigued with the concept—especially because the Mercedes hauler, powered by a 300SL engine, could carry the team's W196 Grand Prix car or 300SLR racer from Stuttgart to Le Mans at 105 miles per hour.

As a former driver, crew chief, and tuner, he saw the Mercedes hauler as something of a challenge. He wanted to build a faster one, one that could haul at up to 112 miles an hour.

Holtkamp started his project with a Mercedes 300 sedan chassis because he believed the electric load-leveling suspension would adjust and keep the ride-height stable. He added Porsche torsion bars

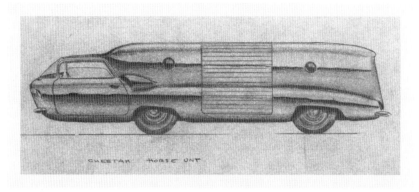

Holtkamp had actually planned a limited production of his transporter, and had even designed a "mini-van" version. But at $16,000 a piece in 1961, he didn't have too many customers beating a path to his door.
James Degnan Collection

that were manually adjustable, but kept the stock Mercedes front and rear axles, spindles, and differential in place.

He purchased the 1960 Chevy El Camino cab new directly from the GM Truck Assembly Plant in Van Nuys, California. The engine he chose came from a 1957 Corvette, hopped up to 300 horsepower, and he mated it with a Chevy three-speed transmission.

The original bodywork (which has changed over the past forty years) was crafted by famed panel beaters Troutman and Barnes of Los Angeles. They made all the body panels, including the full belly pan, from aluminum and designed them to be removable (in as quickly as seven minutes).

Holtkamp finished his creation, the Cheetah, in nine months. He had hoped to begin production of a small number of the haulers, perhaps four or five each year, for weekend racing enthusiasts. But his proposed $16,000 price tag (in 1961!) didn't have racers beating a path to his door.

Holtkamp drove the Cheetah to several West Coast sports car races, hauling the Willment Formula Junior for the Retzloff Racing Team. But he wasn't pleased with the transporter's handling. By one account, Holtkamp once hit the brakes coming down a hill and did a backwards wheelie—the rear wheels came off the ground so far the hauler's nose hit the pavement. It's probably that incident that made him decide to lengthen the wheelbase by a few feet and move the engine rearward toward the center of the vehicle. Sadly, with that change, most of the beautiful Troutman and Barnes bodywork was discarded.

Holtkamp never fully completed the lengthened Cheetah and sold it as a project to California hot rod parts manufacturer Dean Moon sometime in the early 1970s. Moon had the connections and the wherewithal to complete Holtkamp's dream if anyone did. His first planned modification was to replace the Mercedes four-wheel drum brakes with Airheart disc components. That was an ill-fated idea—while the Cheetah was at the Hurst Airheart Company, the 1971 earthquake hit.

Yet maybe fate wasn't so ill-willed. When the earthquake hit, the building literally fell to pieces around the Cheetah, and except for one small dent, the transporter was virtually untouched. The brake conversion was never completed, however, and the Cheetah

Eventually Holtkamp sold his transporter to speed equipment manufacturer Dean Moon. Moon sent the truck to the Hurst Airheart Company for installation of disc brakes. While it was there, the storage building it was in collapsed due to the 1971 Los Angeles earthquake. The transporter, however, did not sustain much damage. *James Degnan Collection*

was eventually moved back to Moon's shop in Santa Fe Springs. There it sat, outside, on jack stands, for about eighteen years.

Degnan's call to Moon Equipment verified that the vehicle was still there. He also learned that Moon had just passed away, and all the stuff in his buildings was being sold off. In no time, Degnan wrote a check to the estate and Holtkamp's creation was his.

"I had my Olds transporter, so we used a forklift and hoisted the Cheetah onto the back of it," he says. "It must have been quite a sight—so unstable that I would only go thirty-five miles per hour on the freeway all the way home. But I was younger then . . ."

After he got it home, Degnan brought it to a mechanic friend who installed power steering, power brakes, rewired it, and dropped in a standard 350-cubic-inch Chevy engine.

The Cheetah now runs and drives, but Degnan isn't quite ready to break any speed records with it. "I'd be hard-pressed to drive it faster than sixty miles per hour," he says. "It was Holtkamp's desire to build a Mercedes beater; one that could haul race cars to the track in record time, but clearly, this car is not it."

The Cheetah has sat for many years in the back of Degnan's shop. The vehicle still needs all the bodywork completed that was discarded when Holtkamp lengthened the chassis. For Degnan, it's a clear case of, "better watch what you wish for, because it might come true." He has the transporter of his dreams, but now what?

The transporter was eventually stored behind Moon's speed shop. At this point, the disc brake conversion was only half completed. Additionally, the transporter was in the process of being lengthened to improve its on-road handling characteristics, but this was never completed. *James Degnan Collection*

CHAPTER EIGHT

Death Be Not Proud

BY KEN GROSS

ADAPTED FROM *RODDER'S JOURNAL,* ISSUE NO. 21

Many readers already know the name Ken Gross for his automotive writing and journalism. While serving as director of the Petersen Automotive Museum in Los Angeles, Ken got wind of a custom Mercury once owned by a hot rodder named Rulon McGregor. Sadly, McGregor was one of hot rodding's early casualties during a dry lake run in 1949. After his death, his custom '39 Mercury was tucked away in his parents' garage and all but forgotten for the next thirty years.

In this unique piece, Gross describes how he acquired McGregor's custom Mercury for the Petersen museum and revisits the hot-rodding scene at the time of the crash that calamitous morning. Here's the story:

Orel T. McGregor just didn't want to part with his son's car. He had parked the '39 Mercury in his rickety garage after his twenty-one-year-old son's funeral in 1949, and it was still there more than thirty years later.

But this time, when Jim Fuller and his friend, Robert Morris, showed up with money in hand in the early 1980s, his wife was ready to part with the Merc and signed over the title. Within minutes, the car was whisked away.

It seemed like almost too easy of a process, considering all the McGregors had been through.

It was a Sunday—May 22, 1949, when their world changed. Their son Rulon was out racing at El Mirage Dry Lake, about 125 miles north and east of Los Angeles, at the edge of the Mojave Desert. At twenty-one, he was a new member of the SCTA RoadRunners hot rod club and was driving a Class C lakester powered by a lusty 276-cubic-inch '42 Mercury flathead.

Starting his return run, he accelerated quickly, moving fast as he went through the course. Crouching low behind the steering wheel, McGregor deliberately kept his head down to minimize wind resistance. Then he nailed the throttle, overcoming some wheelspin as his tires scrabbled for grip on the hard alkalai-laced lakebed surface. Quickly gathering speed, he roared ahead. In less than twenty seconds, he was dead.

On the other side of the course was twenty-two-year-old Robert Fadave, a Gents car club member driving a '40 Ford business coupe as a patrol car. He had stopped to pick up two friends and didn't see that McGregor had begun his return. With wind, lake dust, and morning fog obscuring the view, he still didn't see McGregor when he decided to take a fatal short cut—right through the middle of the race course.

What resulted was a horrendous crash. McGregor's still-accelerating lakester t-boned the coupe squarely in the drivers' side, bounced off the '40 into the air, hung for a moment, rolled over, shed its flimsy body shell, and came to rest on its wire wheels. The hard-hit coupe then flipped, rolled and slid a few feet, and came to rest on its side with nearly every panel damaged. Rulon was killed instantly, so was coupe passenger Jackson Pendleton, also twenty-one. Driver Robert Fadave died from his injuries in the ambulance en route to San Bernadino hospital, fifty-seven miles away through the Cajon Pass. Fadave's other passenger, John Cuthbert, was first taken to that hospital, then transferred to Queen of the Angels Hospital. Whether he survived is unknown.

After the sickening crunch of the crash, many spectators and racers, at first stunned, immediately ran toward the scene of the accident. The lakebed erupted with shouts, screams, and a siren as a big Buick ambulance approached the accident. It was a scene of carnage with car parts and bodies strewn about. Realizing that two men were still barely alive, rescue workers extricated them and placed them into the ambulance for the long run to the hospital.

Lynn Yakel, a frequent Russetta Timing Association competitor in the 1950s, and the owner of one of the coolest chopped and channeled '32 five-windows ever, actually saw the accident happen. "I was driving onto the lake with Frank Leonard and Connie Weidell in a '36 Ford coupe," he says. "The race car was coming back right next to the course and this '40 coupe was cutting across. We all looked over and somebody said, 'What's that asshole doing?' There was a crash and a huge pile of dust. A few seconds later, a wheel came rolling out of the dust cloud."

"People were trying to take pictures," Yakel recalls. "I saw a few cameras smashed. They didn't want pictures of that stuff happening. A lot of time was spent cleaning things up."

"I was sitting near the ambulance," Lee Hammock, another witness, recalls. "And I remember thinking, they're gonna hit! I had my camera because I just loved taking pictures. It was just an impulse. After I took a few pictures, I threw the camera back in the car and tried to help. But there wasn't much anyone could do. When I got back to the scene, one of those guys was lying on the ground, obviously alive, but screaming in pain. As far as the guys inside the lakester and the coupe, there was no question."

Bill Burke, the first hot rodder to build a belly tank, also remembers the tragic scene all too well. "I built that little T for Rulon," he says sadly. "It was a '23 or '24, with a T grille. It had a Model T frame and wire wheels. The engine was a modified flat-head. . . . Accidents took place, but ones like that were rare. In the early days, they didn't have the restrictions they did later. People would drive all over the course."

After it was all over, who could blame the McGregors for putting Rulon's '39 Mercury away and never selling it? And by the time Jim Fuller found out about it, most other enthusiasts had forgotten about the customized classic.

Fuller heard about the car from a friend, when they had been talking about the increasing rarity of custom cars in Monterey Park, California, where such rides once were a dime a dozen. "They're all gone," Fuller said in sadness, but his friend told him, no not quite. There was one left. Fuller paid $300 to get a solid tip to where the chopped Mercury his friend spoke of was, and then went to see it.

When he convinced Mrs. McGregor to part with it, he was surprised as anyone.

He was also surprised by what was under the hood. "The Mercury had a stock engine in it with dual exhausts," Fuller says. "It once had a hopped-up motor, but supposedly McGregor put that in a lakester." The original interior was stock maroon leather, worn and dried out from years of storage. The Carson-padded top needed recovering and the paint was also in rough shape.

Fuller contracted Fran Busey to recover the Carson top with the correct pebbled-grain white fabric. Then he repainted the Mercury dark red. Fuller also installed an up-to-date engine, also a Mercury, but with a four-inch crank, a Winfield SU-1A camshaft, twin carbs, and high-compression heads. He kept the car for about fifteen years and used it very sparingly. "Every time I'd take it out," he says, "it would stop. The gas tank was filled with crud from sitting so long. We finally took it out and cleaned it."

Walter F. Larson, a businessman from Plainview, Texas, bought Fuller's car in 1999, after the two had talked about a sale for years. But when Larson got the car to Texas, he quickly decided it wasn't quite what he wanted.

"I thought I was getting a show car," he explains. "Even with the car's interesting history, which I learned, I was disappointed." So he placed an ad in *Hemmings Motor News* to sell it in the summer of 1999.

When I read that ad in *Hemmings*, I was the executive director of the Petersen Automotive Museum in Los Angeles. I thought the Rulon McGregor Mercury would make a good exhibit car for the museum. After all, it had been California owned and customized the right way for the period. It seemed to be in largely original shape except for the engine, top, and paint freshening, so we struck a deal with Walter Larson that September. It's now at the Petersen Automotive Museum, and when it's not on display, it rests quietly in the Petersen's basement garage, better known as "The Vault," with many other great cars.

McGregor's old Mercury is a great example of a typical custom, before they started chopping big bulbous Mercs and spelling custom with a "K." Sitting inside, you can still see the small black Carson Top Shop plaque on the top header, just to the left of the windshield split. The Mercury's overall condition, while solid, reflects its age so the car still looks very much the way Rulon McGregor built it. It sits on a dropped axle in front and it's been lowered slightly in back. Some chrome has been removed and holes filled. The interior is finished nicely in period style with matching red-and-white tuck and roll. The engine is mildly modified. It's likely that McGregor had more plans for the car, but sadly we'll never know what they were.

Just who was Rulon McGregor? Scant details of his life and passion for fast cars survive among the era's hot-rodding records and participants. He was very active as a lakes racer in the months just before he was killed. His name (misspelled as 'Rulan') appears in results from a September 12, 1948, Russetta meet at El Mirage. Driving for the Stockholders' Car Club in a B roadster, at that meet, he clocked a mid-pack 118.57 miles per hour, beating such notables as Phil Weiand by nearly two miles per hour.

In January 1949, McGregor was pictured (although this time his name is spelled "Rulor") at the National Guard Armory in Los Angeles at the second annual SCTA-sponsored ten-day hot rod exposition. If you look in *Hot Rod* for March 1949, on page ten, you'll see photos of several Road Runner Club members assembling one of two giveaway '32 roadsters at the event. Three members, Rulon McGregor, Bill Burke, and Harvey Haller, are among those pictured and their names are printed on a sign adjacent to the '32 on the stage. This particular Deuce was known as the "Burple" roadster, reflecting the unusual paint color developed by Bill Burke, who was also credited with building the first belly tank. That roadster was won by a Long Beach lady, Mrs. F. C. Bailey. It really makes you wonder, where is that car now?

CHAPTER NINE

My Own Finds
(Over 35 Years of Searching)

When my friend Peter Egan and I drove my newly acquired Cobra across the United States in May 2001, we had a lot of time to talk. And one of those conversations centered around the cars we had owned and the cars we would *like* to own.

Each of us had already owned quite a number of cars, well over 100 cars each. But by the time we had downed our last pint of beer (we were doing our "research" in a Colorado microbrewery), I revealed to Peter something I had never considered before—that except for a couple of those 100-plus cars, none had a for-sale sign attached or had even been for sale when I found them. In fact, nearly every single car I had owned was a barn find.

My first "barn find" was a 1940 Ford convertible, purchased for $25 from behind Charlie's Welding Shop in Rocky Point, New York.

I was fourteen years old, and bought it because Wally's friend Lumpy on the TV show *Leave It to Beaver* drove one and I liked it. My second car, purchased when I was fifteen years old, was a '39 Ford woody that I discovered as it sat next to a barn in Brentwood, New York. Even as a teenager, I began to realize that the best deals could be had on cars that weren't actually for sale.

After thirty-five years of taking this approach, I've found many a treasure. And many of these barn finds helped inspire me to write this book, so what kind of an author would I be if I didn't share some my own stories? Here are the ones I like the best.

Sometimes You Can Go Back Home

In 1969, when I was fifteen years old, my friend Xavier Lucena and I were walking across a schoolyard near his house in Brentwood, Long Island. Through the fence, inside an adjoining yard, I saw an old car, so we walked over to take a closer look. We were two car-crazy kids, so I knew instantly that it was a 1939 Ford DeLuxe Woody Wagon. Of course, this compelled us to walk up to the house and knock on the door. Not that either one of us had two nickels to rub together, but we asked if the car was for sale. The former surf wagon indeed was, for $300.

That night, I told my father about the car, and he came with me to look at it again the following Saturday. It was a nice car—the wood was solid and the car had no rust. A budding surfer myself, I decided I needed that car. But I didn't have $300 and neither did my parents. Yet, I came up with a plan. I asked a woman I often did yard work for to advance me the money; in return, I'd work off my debt all summer. A week later, my father hooked a tow rope to his VW Squareback, and with me behind the wheel of the Ford, we dragged that car twenty miles home.

My father and I were naive auto restorers. We had no tools, no garage, and no experience. So we did what all novice restorers do—we took the woody apart! Little did I know that taking a car apart is easy, but putting it back together costs a lot of money.

Fresh from Charlie's Welding Shop in Rocky Point, New York, I purchased this 1940 Ford DeLuxe convertible for $25 because I fell in love with the car that Lumpy drove on *Leave It to Beaver*. Here, I wrangled some friends into helping me sand the body. *Tom Cotter*

My dad and I toiled on the woody. We spent the summer sanding, bleaching, and varnishing. Then we covered the car in plastic over the winter, only to have to begin the entire process over again in the spring. Eventually, my patience to restore the woody ran out, and against my father's wishes, I sold it in 1973 through *Hemmings Motor News* to a collector in Puerto Rico for $1,250.

Years passed, I finished school, got married, and began a career in motorsports marketing. We moved to NASCAR country in North Carolina and had a son. Still, the desire to own a cool surf wagon was always in the back of my mind. Eventually, my wife, Pat, my high school sweetheart who had helped me sand and varnish the woody, began looking at classified ads for one. Then I had a chance conversation with Thos. Bryant, editor of *Road & Track* magazine. Thos., who owns a Ford woody, told me about the National Woodie Club and the *Woodie Times* magazine. He said there were always woodies for sale in the classified section. So my wife and I joined the club and followed up on a few classified ads. Yet, for one reason or another, we never got very serious about buying a woody.

The way it looked when I purchased it in 1969 for $300 from local surfer, Richie Taylor. My father and I toiled with its restoration for a couple of years before I sold it in 1973 to a car collector in Puerto Rico for $1,250. *Tom Cotter*

Then, one day while I was at work, Pat called me and said that we had just received the new National Woodie Club Membership Roster. She said that there were three members in Puerto Rico, and that two owned 1939 woodies. That evening, by my second phone call, I had found the actual woody that I had sold twenty-six years earlier. The car had passed through two other owners, and it was presently owned by a car-collecting dentist, Ted Lopez, who lived in the town of Ponce. We had a terrific phone conversation, but he told me the car was not for sale. He also mentioned that he was coming up to Charlotte for the huge AutoFair car show and flea market, and that he'd love to meet me and show me photos. We met and began a dialogue over the next two years. In that time, Ted went from "the car is not for sale," to "if I sell the woody, I'll give you first option," to "I think I'm going to sell you the car."

My wife Pat rediscovered the car in 1997, three owners later, but still in Puerto Rico. By that time, my dad was deceased, so I had a real urge to buy the car back. By 1999, the car came home to the United States. I re-purchased it for $13,000. Here it is sitting at the docks in Jacksonville, Florida. *Tom Cotter*

Today the woody is finally restored. I hope to pass the car onto my son, Brian, one day. *Tom Cotter*

Finally, after more than a quarter-century, I was able to buy the car that my dad, now deceased, and I had worked so hard on. When I drove down to Jacksonville, Florida, to trailer the car home, it was quite emotional. Even though the wood was changed to teak from its original maple, the car was complete, and at $13,000, Ted gave me a good deal on it.

Bringing the car home was one challenge; deciding what to do with it was another. Should I restore it or modernize it? After a year of hemming and hawing, I decided to install a modern drivetrain, with the goal of one day driving to California with Pat and my son Brian.

Many car enthusiasts I meet curse themselves for selling the car they drove in high school or college, and I was certainly among them. But I got to be one of the lucky car nuts who made up for his mistake and bought that great car back again. I'm certainly a lucky guy.

OWNERSHIP OF A CAR OPENS UP OPPORTUNITIES TO FIND OTHERS
In 2001, I achieved a lifelong dream: ownership of a 289 Cobra. Ever since 1965, when I was in fifth grade, I had dreamed of owning a Cobra. But my finances and the car's escalating value were always out of sync, until 2000. That's when I sold my motorsports marketing/public relations agency to a conglomerate, and promptly informed my wife Pat that it was "Cobra Time."

After months of searching and considering numerous Cobras, I purchased Cobra CSX2490 in Walnut Creek, California. With friend Peter Egan along for the ride, I drove it 3,000 miles across the country to my home in North Carolina. Peter documented the trip in an excellent story that was featured in the February 2002 issue of *Road & Track* magazine.

Soon after the *Road & Track* story hit the newsstands, I got a call from a neighbor of mine whom I had never actually met. Hugh Barger owns the 500-acre cattle farm on the other side of the fence from my own property. "Hello, Tom, this is your neighbor Hugh Barger," he said. "I just read about your A.C. Cobra, and wondered if I could take a look at it. We seem to have something in common."

I passed this barn on the way to the office for twenty years, but never really imagined it actually contained an old car. From the road, I could barely see the tractor peaking out. *Tom Cotter*

I agreed to drive the Cobra to his home, about a half-mile from my house, on Saturday morning.

My wife Pat, son Brian, and I had a wonderful time visiting with Hugh and Brenda Barger when Hugh asked if I'd like to see what he had inside one of his barns. Now, I had driven past the Barger's barns for nearly two decades, and like all old car enthusiasts, had fantasized about what might lurk inside. But I've peered into too many old barns and been disappointed when I found it contained only an old manure spreader or a twenty-year-old pile of hay instead of a Porsche 550 Spyder. Still, the dream of a barn find is a constant fantasy, so Brian and I eagerly followed Hugh out to the barn to see what he had to show us.

My disappointment was only mild when I saw a '60s Alfa Romeo Giulia GT inside the doorway. Hugh said to pardon the mess,

243

As I walked up with Hugh
Barger, I was only mildly
impressed in the Alfa
Romeo that Hugh figured
had sat there for about
twenty-five years.
Obviously the tree wasn't
there when it was parked.
Tom Cotter

and that the Alfa had been in the barn for about twenty-five years.
It wasn't the Alfa that Hugh wanted me to see, but the car behind
the Alfa. Peering into the dark and dusty barn, I could see a familiar,
but unidentifiable, silhouette of a sports car.

"In the 1960s, my father sold my Alvis, and he bought me this
A.C. Greyhound to drive to graduate school," he said. "Brenda and I
used it for years when we lived near Washington, D.C. But when we
moved back to Davidson, it wasn't the most reliable car, so I just
decided to park the thing. I guess it's been in the barn for at least
thirty-five years."

I was flabbergasted. Here, in my neighbor's barn, was a car that
rolled off the very same A.C. assembly line in Thames Ditton,
England, as my own beloved Cobra. Unbelievable.

For those unfamiliar with the Greyhound, it has Cobra-like lines,
but is an aluminum fastback coupe rather than a roadster. It shares the
same grille as a 289 Cobra and was designed to be A.C.'s new model as
the company attempted to depart from the Aceca coupe style. The
Greyhound seats four and is unlike the 289 Ford-powered Cobras in

that it is powered by an exquisite six-cylinder Bristol engine that had actually been developed by BMW before World War II.

Brian and I tried to see the car as best we could, but the barn was very dark, the confines were tight, and there were inches of dust on the car. "I'm sorry it's such a mess," Hugh said. "I hope there are no rats living in it." Indeed, the car had seen better days; it had sunken down to the chassis into the dirt floor.

As we said goodbye to Hugh and Brenda, they invited us back with flashlights anytime if we wanted to get a better look. Of course, even though I didn't need it, I had to ask Hugh if he'd sell me the Greyhound. "Well, Brenda has been nagging me for years to push it into a ditch, but the car is not in my way, and it doesn't cost me anything to keep it, so I think I'll just hold on to it."

Nobody could have ever convinced me—of all people—that there was an A.C. in my neighbor's barn. Never. But there was, so I'm more eager now than ever to look inside every old barn and garage I see. I still live the dream of finding a real Cobra in a barn.

A SPRITE-LY VETERAN OF SEBRING, LE MANS

I was in Portland, Oregon, on business in the summer of 2004, and decided to give my old pal Stan Huntley a call. Stan was one of the most insane car collectors I had ever met, and I mean that as a good thing. I first met Stan in the early 1990s because of a story that *Road & Track* had written years earlier about him and his road racing Morris Minor pickup truck. That's right: folks in the Pacific Northwest regularly witnessed a lowly Morris truck embarrassing more traditional sports cars, such as MGs, Triumphs, and Porsches. Anyway, Stan and I became friends as I was constructing my own Morris sedan racer.

When I called him last summer, he seemed much more somber than excited. He said to he had to talk to me in person, and he sounded serious. When I arrived, Stan told me of his cancer and that he was dying. "I'm not laughing anymore about those bumper stickers that say: He Who Dies With The Most Toys Wins," he told me, referencing his sizable, and very eclectic, car collection. He had hot rods, sports cars, and race cars, including that giant-killer Morris pickup and the very first MGB ever built, but he also had one car that I had always been interested in owning.

"Now's your chance to own that Sprite," he announced as I sat in his living room. Of course, I knew which one he referred to: a 1965 Austin-Healey Sprite prototype coupe, Serial No. HAN8-R-143, that the factory Healey racing team had entered at Sebring and Le Mans. "I'd like to sell it to you now, so that Pat (Stan's wife) won't have to deal with it later," he said.

The Sprite resembled an eighty-percent scale Cobra Daytona Coupe, also made of aluminum, but was powered by an A-Series

I had always been interested in my friend Stan Huntley's 1965 Austin-Healey Le Mans prototype. When he knew his cancer was terminal, he asked if I would like to be the car's next caretaker. *Tom Cotter*

1275-cc Sprite engine. The car was painted fluorescent orange when it raced at Sebring that year, but when it was brought to Le Mans a few months later, the French organizers threatened to disqualify it because the color was so bright. They thought it would be a distraction to other drivers. (Of course, that's exactly why Geoffrey Healey painted the car orange—so the Ford GT40s, which could pass the Sprite in excess of 100 miles per hour faster, would notice the diminutive cars.) So it was quickly painted British Racing Green for the French twenty-four-hour race. Then, after a couple of years as a club racer, the car was purchased by Stan. He put it into his garage, and even though it was his intention to restore and race it, the car sat idle for nearly thirty years. The odometer of this

The coupe is pure Austin-Healey Sprite underneath, but has all-aluminum bodywork on top. The car ran as a factory racer at Sebring and Le Mans in 1965 and 1966. *Tom Cotter*

Serial No. HAN-8-R-143 was part of a two-car team at Le Mans in 1966, and ran as high as 16th until retiring with oil leaks. *Tom Cotter*

forty-year-old car read 4,341 miles; most of those miles were accumulated during its Le Mans twenty-four-hour, Sebring twelve-hour, and Daytona twenty-four-hour appearances.

I feel fortunate to have been chosen to be the next caretaker of this rare international racer. The car is being authentically restored by my friends Billy Coates and David Brown in its brilliant orange color scheme and will be vintage raced in Monterey, Sebring, and Daytona vintage events. Hopefully, it will also make it to the Goodwood and Le Mans historic events one day. I had been interested in owning that car for nearly twenty years, and I feel privileged that Stan chose me to bring it out of retirement.

Stan passed away in early 2005, but there are a slew of his friends and relatives who will have tears in their eyes when they see that car return to the track . . . and I'll be one of them.

248

CHAPTER TEN

Sleeping Beauties

PHOTOGRAPHY BY HERBERT W. HESSELMANN

Reprinted with permission from Automobile Quarterly,
Vol. 22, No. 2.

I read the following story in Automobile Quarterly *when it was published in the early 1980s. I was intrigued with the almost perverted beauty of these rotting classics. It started me thinking that maybe not every Bugatti or Cord needs to be restored, but maybe every once in a while a car of this sort should be allowed to slowly return to dust. I fell in love with these photographs, and couldn't stop looking at every detail: the moss growing on the Alfa Romeo, the dandelion growing from the Lancia windowsill. A poster series was offered by* Automobile Quarterly, *which I desperately wanted. But at the time, money was tight, and I couldn't justify the purchase. Today, a quarter-century*

later, I'd still love to find a set of those posters to surround myself with these incredible "Sleeping Beauties."

I saved the story as my all-time favorite "barn-find piece," and its imagery helped to inspire this book. Though the cars it describes may be out of reach, there's something optimistic here too—a link from present to past and a sense of the automobile's organic place in our lives.

I am so thankful that the fine folks at Automobile Quarterly *have allowed this story and a couple of the photographs to appear again.*

—TOM COTTER

"If only . . . ." One leans back and imagines all the lost opportunities in life. A lover long since departed, but never forgotten. The job offer refused. The letter left unsent. Of course, there is nothing to be done; the vile worm of time continues inexorably forward. And yet someone or something has given us the terrible gift of nostalgia. "If only . . . "

From left: Cord 812, ca. 1937; Bugatti Type 57 coupe, ca. 1935–1938; Bugatti Type 5 coupe, ca. 1932–1935

Cord L29, ca. 1929–1930

Lancia Flaminia GT, ca. 1959

Tatra 600 Tatraplan, ca. 1947–1951

251

A casual glance at the classifieds of just a decade ago reveals some bleak realities about missed opportunities. A Cobra goes begging for $12,000, a Ferrari Lusso seeks a buyer at only $8,500, a Corvette for a song, a Jaguar for a pittance. During the Depression, it must have been even worse as the vanquished playboys resigned

Jowett Javelin, ca. 1952 (front); Alfa Romeo Type 6C2500 C, ca. 1948–1950 (left), which ran in the 1950 Mille Miglia and Targa Florio and is one of three built. Bugatti "Fiacre" Type 44, ca. 1927, is on the right.

Bugatti Type 57 Altante coupe, ca. 1935–1938

Panhard Dynamic "Junior" ca. 1936, (left); Bentley Mark VI, ca. 1946–1951 (right)

Graham Paige Series 116 Supercharger Six (interior)

Graham Paige Series 116 Supercharger Six, ca. 1937

their elegant playthings for a fistful of bills. Though the dollars they sought were much more powerful than those of the present day, the prices they asked are still low enough to make us weep. "If only. . . "

The photographs on these pages are yet another case in point. Rusting, rotting, and decaying, these "sleeping beauties" will never be awakened by the restorer's kiss. Their owner has acquired them as if they were stray cats, unwanted and unloved. For most he paid practically nothing. Some were even gifts. And none will ever be sold.

We cannot tell you the precise location of this sirens' graveyard. We know only that it is located somewhere in Europe. German photographer Herbert Hesselmann is one of the lucky who have been allowed to enter this hallowed crypt.

Though worthy of poetry, we present these death masks with identification but without comment. Many of the faces are familiar, most would be priceless if restored today. Yet they lie sleeping peacefully, perhaps forever.

Index

Got a great car find story? Send it in!

If you have great stories about cars found in unusual places that you'd like to have considered for inclusion in the follow-up to *The Cobra in the Barn*, send a brief description of the car found and why the story of its discovery is unique to the author at the address below:

c/o Tom Cotter
MBI Publishing Company
380 Jackson Street
Suite 200
St. Paul, MN 55101

Or send e-mail to: tomgcotter@adelphia.net